Actor's Dictionary

3000+
Industry Terminology for American Film,
Multimedia, Television, and Theater
(First Edition)

Plus, how to create an actor's resume, find
agents and auditions, and look like a *pro*
during interviews, auditions, and on the set.

*BONUS: A Description of the 30 Most Popular
American Entertainment Awards Shows/Presentations*

Edited by
LeeAnne Krusemark
Copyright 2018
All Rights Reserved
ISBN-10#197818722X
ISBN-13#978-197818221

TABLE OF CONTENTS

TABLE OF CONTENTS
(Continued)

*"All the world's a stage.
And all the men and women merely players."*
~ William Shakespeare

"Theater is life with the dull bits cut out."
~ Alfred Hitchcock

"Acting is behaving truthfully under imaginary circumstances."
~ Sanford Meisner

*"Acting should be bigger than life.
Scripts should be bigger than life.
It should all be bigger than life."*
~ Bette Davis

*"I don't think actors should ever expect to get a role,
because the disappointment is too great."*
~ Al Pacino

*"If you apply reason and logic to this career,
you're not going to get very far."*
~ Sydney Poitier

"The most important thing the actor has to work on is his mind."
~ Stella Adler

"Find out who you are and be that person."
Ellen Degeneres

*"Create the highest, grandest vision possible for your life, because
you become what you believe."*
Oprah Winfrey

*"Acting is not about being someone different.
It's finding the similarity in what is apparently different,
then finding myself in there."*
~ Meryl Streep

Introduction: Whether you're heading to your first audition or your first stage or screen set, knowing the industry lingo can be crucial to landing an acting job, keeping the one you have, or ever getting another one. Not understanding the words, slang, and phrases used daily on the set and in the entertainment industry can cause miscommunication between you and the director, the production crew and everyone else, including the seasoned actors, and can label you as an unprofessional amateur, resulting in bad relationships, and decreasing your chances of getting hired again. Some of these phrases have been passed on for generations and there is a good chance that you'll hear most or all of this acting jargon during your career. I've also included a section on finding an agent and/or a manager, finding and landing an audition, and information about all of the most popular American entertainment awards shows. Everyone has to start somewhere, and the best somewhere to start is here! PS. If you think you don't need to know any of this to succeed, remember: they will test you on the way up, they will praise you at the top, and they will love to hate you on the way back down, all depending on how you treated them along the way in this business we call show.

Break a Leg, LeeAnne Krusemark, Editor

Phraseology Examples & Translations

Ex. - At the **Audition**: Stand on your **Mark** next to the **Flat** for a **Cold Reading** for an upcoming **Under 5 Role**.

Translation: During your tryout for a role that will have five lines or less, you are to stand on a specific point next to the wood frame covered with stretched cloth and read lines you are unfamiliar with.

Ex. - On the **Slate**: **Wild Line Pick-up Take one A, B & C**.

Translation: On the information chalkboard: The actor will read the line three times without interruption by the director.

Ex. - From the **AD** to the **2nd AD**: "Get an **Apple Box** on the **Set** for the **Abby Singer**, but make sure it's removed quickly for the **Martini** because we've almost reached the **Golden Time**."

Translation: The assistant director tells the second assistant director to get a crate for an actor to stand on for the second to last shot of the day, but have it removed for the last shot of the day because the extras have been on the set for almost 16 hours, after which they will be paid a much higher rate per hour.

Ex. - From the **2nd AD** to the **2nd 2nd AD/3rd AD**: "Get the **Principal** some water because there were too many **Clicks and Pops** in the last **Take**."

Translation: The second assistant director tells the second second assistant director to get the actor water because there were too many clicking sounds caused by dry mouth during filming.

Sometimes, even the definitions use terminology you may at first be unfamiliar with.

Ex. - **Cut and Hold**: The **Final Take** for this **Scene** where the **Camera Operator** is **Checking the Gate** to be certain the film is **In the Can** to call a **Wrap**.

Translation: Once the director is done filming, everyone will hold their positions while the person in charge of camera shots checks to make sure everything was filmed properly so the director can then dismiss the cast.

Actor's Dictionary

(Each letter/number is considered a
separate unit and alphabetized accordingly.)

# #

#1 Bar, Number 1 Bar: The lighting bar immediately behind the proscenium arch or the front bar that hangs over the stage in a non-proscenium arch theater.

1st AD: *See First Assistant Director.*

1st Position (2nd, 3rd, etc.): The place marked for the actor to start or stop on.

10 out of 12: A contractual term for an actor or crew when there can only be 10 hours of work during a 12 hour period.

10-1: Slang term for bathroom.

18 to Look Younger, 18 to Play Younger: Using a performer who is at least 18 years old to play someone under 18.

180° Rule, 180-Degree Rule: Action must move across the screen in the same direction in sequence in order to preserve continuity. *(Also known as Imaginary Line)*

2nd AD: *See Second Assistant Director.*

2nd 2nd AD: *See Second Second Assistant Director.*

2-S, 2-SHOT, Two Shot (3, 4, etc.): Designates how many people are in the shot.

3 Major Meanings: The three passions of a character that give them their core purpose in life. *(Also known as Major Meanings)*

3rd AD: *See Third Assistant Director.*

30-Mile Zone, Thirty-Mile Zone (TMZ): The reasonable distance that union workers should be expected to travel to a production. *(Also known as Studio Zone)*

3/4, Three Quarter Shot: This camera shot frames a person from the knees up.

4As: *See American Association of Actors and Artistes.*

47: Slang for a clothespin used as props or to hang props. *(Also known as Ammo or Bullet or C-47 or CP47 or Peg)*

8 by 10, 8x10: A headshot of a performer based on the dimensions of the photo.

A

Abby, Abby Singer: The next to last shot of the day. Besides his work as an AD and UPM and his contributions to the DGA, Abby Singer is best known for the shot he coined which saves time on sets by notifying crew the end of filming is near.

ABC-Take: Three different takes of a line, usually used for voiceover.

Above the Line: Refers to money budgeted for creative talent, such as actors, writers, directors, and producers.

Above the Title: At the beginning of a movie or show, and in advertisements, when the performer's name appears before the title.

Abstract Setting: A stage setting that does not attempt to present a realistic stage picture.

AC: *See Assistant Cameraman.*

Academic Theater: Theater connected with school and having educational rather than commercial goals. The physical stage may be anything from a classroom to a full-size proscenium arch theater.

Academy Awards: An annual American awards ceremony hosted by the Academy of Motion Picture Arts and Sciences (AMPAS) to recognize excellence in cinematic achievements in the film industry. *(Also known as the Oscars)*

Academy of Motion Picture Arts and Sciences (AMPAS): A professional honorary organization of approximately 6,000 industry professionals worldwide with the goal of advancing the arts and sciences of motion pictures. The Academy is known primarily for its presentation of the annual Academy Awards/Oscars. *(See Appendix: ENTERTAINMENT INDUSTRY ASSOCIATIONS/ORGANIZATIONS)*

Academy of Television Arts (ATAS): A nonprofit organization devoted to the advancement of telecommunication arts and sciences. *(See Appendix: ENTERTAINMENT INDUSTRY ASSOCIATIONS/ORGANIZATIONS)*

Academy Museum of Motion Pictures: A museum by AMPAS in the historic May Company Building on Wilshire Boulevard in Los Angeles. *(See Appendix: ENTERTAINMENT INDUSTRY ASSOCIATIONS/ORGANIZATIONS)*

Accent Lighting: Lighting that stresses certain stage areas. It may be done with intensity and/or color.

Accepting: In improv, embracing the offers made by other performers in order to advance the scene.

ACE: *See American Cinema Editors.*

Acetate Dub: An individually cut record, as opposed to pressed records.

Acousmetre: A sound that is heard but not seen, as in an off-screen sound.

Acoustics: The science of sound as applied to theaters, relating to how sound travels and reverberates.

Across the Board: When an agent represents an actor for film, television, multimedia, commercials, voiceovers and modeling.

Act: One of the main sections of a screenplay or a play. Or, to behave in a certain manner, such as perform.

Act Curtain: A curtain behind the fireproof curtain, and behind the grand drape, if there is one, closing the proscenium opening, and raised or drawn to reveal the stage during an act or scene.

Act Drop: Any front cloth or tabs lowered during intervals, especially used in pantomime and musicals.

Acting: To live truthfully under given imaginary circumstances, as in a performance.

Acting Area: That area within the performance space where the actor may move in full view of the audience. Or, a specific portion of such an area actually used for acting during all or part of a performance.

Acting Bug: A term used to indicate that someone of any age has been infected with a great desire to be an actor.

Acting Edition: Script containing detailed stage directions and additional information, such as prop and wardrobe lists and descriptions of the set.

Acting Process: Specific choices an actor makes to bring the character to life. The specific techniques, methods and tools that an actor uses to be able to live truthfully in an imaginary circumstance. *(Also known as Process)*

Acting Resume: Focuses exclusively on acting and establishes your credibility by listing your acting experience and training used to promote you as an actor to agents and casting directors. *(See Appendix: ACTOR'S RESUME)*

Action: A director's cue to begin filming or start the scene.

Actioning: The rehearsal technique of breaking the text up into its component units, and finding the right action to play at each of those moments.

Actions: The action verbs the actor uses to fulfill the objective. *(Also known as Driving Question or Essential Action or Intention or Motivating Drive or Objective)*

Active: A piece of circuitry is active if it needs a power supply for it to function.

Activity: A specific physical task that may or may not be connected to an action, such as a character loading a gun or packing a suitcase.

Actor: In the past a male performer, now a male or female performer.

Actor Proof: A play or sketch that is almost impervious to bad acting. Francis Swan's Out of the Frying Pan, a hit on Broadway in the 1940s and a staple of community and academic theater ever since, has such ingratiating characters, such a tightly constructed plot, and so much fun and goodwill built into it that it can survive the most amateurish production.

Actor's Agreement: Union contract for hiring an actor for a job.

Actors Equity Association (AEA): Founded in 1913, also known as Equity, the US labor union that represents more than 50,000 actors and stage managers. Equity negotiates wages, working conditions, and provides a wide range of benefits, including health and pension plans. Actors Equity is a member of the AFL-CIO and is affiliated with FIA, an international organization of performing arts unions. *(See Appendix: ENTERTAINMENT INDUSTRY ASSOCIATIONS/ ORGANIZATIONS)*

the Actor's Fund: A nonprofit charitable organization that assists American entertainment and performing arts professionals through a broad spectrum of programs.

Actor's Resume: Focuses exclusively on acting and establishes your credibility by listing your acting experience and training used to promote you as an actor to agents and casting directors. *(See Appendix: ACTOR'S RESUME)*

ACTRA: *See Alliance of Canadian Cinema, Television, and Radio Artists.*

Actress: A female performer.

Actual Call: The heading on the audition sign-in sheet where you write the scheduled time of your audition.

Act Warning: A stage manager's call to actors and crew to announce the time remaining before the beginning of an act, or scene.

AD: *See Assistant Director.*

Adaptation: The action or process of adapting from a written work, typically a novel, into a movie, television or multimedia drama, or stage play.

AD Box: A room on set used as an office where the assistant directors can take care of paperwork, etc.

Additional Camera: An extra camera operator, often needed for complicated action sequences.

Adjudication: Evaluating a production entered into a theater festival or other competition, by a group of people with a wide range of training and experience.

Adjustment: A direction or modification an actor makes in the playing of material. Adjustments are often instructions given by the director. Or, an artist's pay is being increased above the base rate.

Ad Lib: Dialogue in the scene that has been improvised that is not in the script.

Administration: The supervision of all financial, copyright and contractual aspects of either an entire catalog or a particular song.

Ad Pub: Relating to the advertising and publicity department of a motion picture studio.

ADR: *See Automated Dialogue Replacement.*

Advance: Money that has been paid to secure somebody's work, paid before the recording or release of a song or movie, to be deducted against future royalties.

Advance Bar: Lighting bar positioned just downstage of the proscenium arch.

Advance Man: A representative in charge of business arrangements who proceeds a touring company.

Advancing: The process of moving the scene forwards.

AEA: *See Actors Equity Association.*

Aerial: A shot taken from a crane, plane, or helicopter, but is not necessarily a moving shot.

Aesthetic Distance: The maintaining of artistic illusion by sufficient physical or other separation or detachment.

Affective Memory: Memory that involves the actor personally, so that deeply rooted emotional experiences can be relived in the performance. *(Also known as Remembered Emotion)*

AFI: *See American Film Institute.*

AFM: *See American Federation of Musicians.*

Afterpiece: A short performance after the principal one.

AFTRA: *See American Federation of Television and Radio Artists.*

Against Type: Playing a different sort of character than expected.

Agency: The company that employs agents.

Agent: A performer's representation in the business responsible for negotiations and other business deals. *(See Appendix: TIPS TO FINDING AN AGENT, SURVIVING AN INTERVIEW, GETTING AN AUDITION, AND LANDING THE PART)*

Age Range: The range of ages which the actor can realistically play, such as 14-17, 20-30, etc.

Agon: A performance debate.

Airbrushing: A photographic process whereby certain flaws in a picture are gently blown off of a master print.

Air Checking: Having a television or multimedia performance professionally taped.

Aisle: A walkway that goes through two different seat areas.

Alan Smithee: The pseudonym used by directors who refuse to put their name on a film and want to disassociate themselves, usually when they believe their control or vision has been corrupted by the studio.

Alienation Effect: Allows the audience to reflect critically and intellectually on the themes and problems of the play.

A-List: Top-tier actors, but can also refer to producers, directors and writers who can be guaranteed to have a film made and released.

Allegorical Characters: These characters are symbolic, set, and stoney with no possibility of change.

Allegory: A dramatic work or a portion of one that expresses meaning by means of personification and symbolism (i.e., characters may be named Everyman, Lust, Greed, Death, etc.).

Alley Staging: The staging of a performance with the audience placed on two sides, as though the performance space is a street. *(Also known as Avenue Staging or Tennis-Court Staging)*

Alliteration: The repetition of consonant sounds at the beginning of words.

Alternate: One or two actors who alternate in a specific role. Or, an understudy.

Amateur: A person who acts without pay.

Amateur Rights, Amateur Royalty: Permission from the playwright to produce the play by a theater company whose participants may work without salary. In some cases a flat royalty is charged based on theater seating capacity, average ticket price, and the number of performances.

Amateur Theater: Non-professional theater, where people usually perform without pay.

Ambient Sound: Any non-verbal and non-musical sound within a scene. This includes artificial sounds and silence.

AMC: *See a Minor Consideration.*

Am Dram: Abbreviation for Amateur Dramatics, meaning non-professional productions.

American Association of Actors and Artistes (4A's): A member of the AFL-CIO and a few of the individual unions are not. The current AAAA member unions of the AFL-CIO are: AEA, AGMA, GIAA, and SAG-AFTRA. *(See Appendix: ENTERTAINMENT INDUSTRY ASSOCIATIONS/ORGANIZATIONS)*

American Cinema Editors (ACE): An honorary society of film editors that are voted in based on the qualities of professional achievements, their education of others, and their dedication to editing. *(See Appendix: ENTERTAINMENT INDUSTRY ASSOCIATIONS/ORGANIZATIONS)*

American College Theater Festival: An annual competition of college and university productions that begins in local areas and advances to state, regional, and national festivals, sponsored by the American Theater Association.

American Federation of Musicians of the United States and Canada (AFM): The largest organization of musicians in the world, with more than 80,000 musicians. *(See Appendix: ENTERTAINMENT INDUSTRY ASSOCIATIONS/ORGANIZATIONS)*

American Federation of Television and Radio Artists (AFTRA): The union that represented performers for work in radio and television, now merged with the Screen Actors Guild to become SAG-AFTRA. *(See Screen Actors Guild)*

American Film Institute (AFI): A nonprofit educational arts organization that preserves the legacy of the first 100 years of American film. AFI honors movie, television, and multimedia artists and their work by hosting a variety of annual events. *(See Appendix: ENTERTAINMENT INDUSTRY ASSOCIATIONS/ORGANIZATIONS)*

American Shot: Getting its name from the westerns of the 1930-40s to show the actor's gun holsters, this shot frames from mid-thighs up. *(Also known as Cowboy)*

American Two Shot: A shot that shows the two heads facing each other in profile to the camera.

Ammo: Slang for a clothespin used as props or to hang props. *(Also known as 47 or Bullet or C-47 or CP47 or Peg)*

AMPAS: *See Academy of Motion Picture Arts and Sciences.*

Amphitheater: Originally the Colosseum in Rome, now any large, oval-shaped building with no roof and tiers of spectator seats.

Amplifier: A piece of equipment which amplifies or increases the sound captured by a microphone.

Amplitude: The loudness of the sound.

Anachronism: In the course of a stage production, a person or thing that is out of place chronologically.

Angel, Angel Investor: The financial backer of a production who has no creative control.

Angle: The position and view of the camera.

Angle On: A type of shot. This usually occurs in scenes taking place in large settings.

Animal work: Sensory and body work based on the observation of animals, birds and reptiles.

Animation: The process of creating the illusion of motion by creating individual frames, as opposed to filming naturally occurring action at a regular frame rate.

Announced: The production has been announced and greenlit, but top-level talent is still being recruited, or the initial script is still being written.

Answer Print: The first graded print of a film that combines sound and picture, which is created for the client to view and approve.

Antagonist: A person or a situation that opposes another character's, usually the protagonist's goals or desires.

Anticipate: To react too soon.

Anti-Climax: A point in a dramatic piece, after the climax, which may emphasize the meaning of the climax by some lesser tension.

Anti-Naturalism: An acting style where the audience is kept aware that they are watching a performance rather than reality. *(Also known as Brechtian Acting)*

Anti-timing: A failing of some actors who seem to be too slow or too fast in responding to action or dialogue on stage.

Antithesis: An opposition in the story used to express confusion and conflict.

A Page: A revised page that extends beyond the original page, going onto a second page (i.e., Page 1, 1A, 2, 3, 3A).

Aperture: A measure of the width of the opening allowing light to enter a camera.

Appear: To act, as in a play or a part.

Applause: The positive response to a performance, in the form of clapping hands.

Apple Boxes: Wooden crates that elevate either an actor or furniture on a set.

Application: A copyrighted work cannot be produced legally until you receive written permission from the author's representative.

Apprentice: A person who serves without pay in an acting company in order to learn about acting or other aspects of theatrical work.

Apron: The area of the stage located directly in front of the proscenium arch. *(Also known as the Forestage)*

Arbor: The metal frame that holds the counterweights.

Arbor Pit: An open slot in the stage floor below the rigging wall that allows the counterweight arbors to travel lower than the stage floor.

Arc: A shot where a moving camera circles around the subject being photographed.

Arch: An opening in a piece of scenery, representing an arch or a space of some other shape intended to remain empty or to be filled with a door, window, etc.

Archetype: A character, place, or thing, that is repeatedly presented in films with a particular style or characterization.

A&R Director: Record company staffer or liaison in charge of selecting new artists, songs and masters.

Arena: A type of stage where the audience is seated on three sides. Or, an open space at floor level in the middle of an auditorium.

Aria: A solo piece written for a main character, focusing on their emotion.

Aristotle's Six Elements of Drama: In his Poetico, Aristotle defines and discusses the six elements that make up the tragedy, which are plot, character, diction, thought, spectacle (scenic effect), and song (music), of which the first two are primary. *(Also known as Six Elements of Tragedy)*

Armorer: A person who is responsible for weapons on the set of a movie, television, or multimedia show.

A-Roll: The primary footage for non-narrative or interview based film, and usually refers to talking heads or footage that directly relates to the moment.

Arrange: To adapt a score for orchestral use.

Arrangement: The adaptation of a composition for performance by other instruments and voices than originally intended.

Arranger: One who adapts a musical work to particular instruments or voices.

Arras: A drape curtain loosely suspended across a stage. Or, a curtain or tapestry used to screen a door, or serving as a wall hanging.

Art Director: A person responsible for designing a film set. *(Also known as Production Designer)*

Articulation: The clear and precise pronunciation of words.

Artificial Sound: The film term for non-instrumental sound effects.

Artist: A person who practices any of the various creative arts, such as a sculptor, painter, writer, actor, or filmmaker, etc.

Artist in Residence: A person from the professional theater, employed for a specified period to train others in acting or other theater arts.

Artist Manager, Artist Representative: An agent who represents artists by publicizing their talents, finding jobs for them, negotiating their contracts and handling other business matters for them.

Aside: A line delivered to audience that isn't meant to be heard by other performers on the stage, often delivered directly to the audience or themselves.

As If: Using the actor's imagination to create emotional reality, as in using the creative over the personal emotional experience philosophy.

Ask-For: In improv, the question asked of the audience in order to start a scene.

ASM: *See Assistant Stage Manager.*

Aspect Ratio: Width to height ratio of film.

Aspirational Type: Casting someone that the viewer can aspire to be: someone of very good looks and fitness, with an air of success and health, but not so glamorous that viewers could never imagine themselves in the actor's place.

Assignment: The transfer of rights to a song or catalog from one copyright proprietor to another.

Assistant Director: Director's assistant, often referred to as the AD, usually tracks daily progress against the filming production schedule, arranges logistics, prepares daily call sheets, checks cast and crew, and maintains order on the set.

Assistant Stage Manager (ASM): Stage manager's assistant, usually responsible for attending production meetings, running rehearsals, clerical organization, and insuring the smooth execution of the performances.

Association of Talent Agents (ATA): Trade association representing more than 100 agencies in Los Angeles and New York. *(See Appendix: ENTERTAINMENT INDUSTRY ASSOCIATIONS/ ORGANIZATIONS)*

Asychronism: Purposeful opposition between sound and image.

ATA: *See Association of Talent Agents.*

ATAS: *See Academy of Television Arts and Sciences*

At Liberty: Having no current acting engagement, out of work, available for casting.

Atmosphere: Another term for extras or background artists. Or, the feeling that a story conveys to readers.

At Rise: Who and what are onstage when the curtain opens.

Audience: People watching the performance.

Audition: A formally arranged session for an actor to display their talents to a casting director, director or producers. *(See Appendix: TIPS TO FINDING AN AGENT, SURVIVING AN INTERVIEW, GETTING AN AUDITION, AND LANDING THE PART)*

Auditorium: The part of the theater where the audience sits. Or, a building that houses the performance.

Auteur: A director who is actively involved in all aspects of filming.

Author: The person who writes the script.

Automated Dialogue Replacement (ADR): Dialogue that has been added in post-production. Automatic digital recording, or additional dialogue recording.

Avail: A courtesy extended by a performer or agent to a producer indicating availability to work a certain job. Avails have no legal or contractual status.

Available Light: The light present on set, discounting lighting equipment set up explicitly for filming.

Avenue Staging: The staging of a performance with the audience placed on two sides of the audience. *(Also known as Alley Staging or Tennis-Court Staging)*

Awards Shows: Groups, organizations, and festivals that recognize achievements in the arts have annual presentations of awards, usually in the form of a sculpture trophy. *(See Bonus: AWARDS SHOWS/PRESENTATIONS)*

B

Babu Spotlight: A small spotlight used at a short distance to give sharp illumination to an actor's face, or to a limited portion of the acting area.

Back: The area behind the set or that part of the stage that is not visible to the audience, including dressing rooms, shops, and offices. *(Also known as Backstage)*

Backcloth: Large piece of cloth, often with scenery or buildings painted on it, that is hung at the back of a stage while a play is being performed. *(Also known as Backdrop)*

Back Door Pilot: A television or multimedia movie, or an episode of an existing series that is a setup for a television or multimedia series of its own if ratings warrant further production. *(Also known as Planted Spin Off)*

Backdrop: Large piece of cloth, often with scenery or buildings painted on it, that is hung at the back of a stage while a play is being performed. *(Also known as Backcloth)*

Back End: Payment on a project when profits are realized.

Backer: A person who invests in a prospective production.

Background (b.g., Bg, BG): Another term for extras or atmosphere, who work in the background of the scene.

Background Action: The signal the Director or AD gives to establish that it is time for the extras to start moving.

Background Breakdown: A list of the background needed (types, age, race, etc.) which includes specific dates they will be needed.

Background Music: The film term for music coming from off-screen.

Background Talent: A term for extras.

Backing: Scenic piece behind an opening in the set, such as a winder, which hides the technical areas beyond. Or, the money invested in a production.

Backing Flat: A flat that stands behind a window or door on the set.

Backlighting: The use of lighting instruments above and behind performers to accent the performers and set them apart from the background.

Backline: The back of the actual stage.

Back of House (BOH): The parts of the theater behind the proscenium, or behind the stage setting.

Backlot: A portion of the studio lot used for exterior shooting which may include undeveloped land.

Back Piece: A wig for the back of the head only.

Backstage: Part of the theater not being seen by the audience, such as dressing rooms. *(Also known as Back)*

Back-Stepping: Direction to an actor to step backward out of frame and count the steps in order to return to the mark.

Backstory: Events imagined to have happened to the character prior to the events of the script, particularly those most relevant to the present story.

Back-to-One: Direction for the performers to go back to their starting positions at the beginning of the scene. *(Also known as From the Top or Reset, or To Ones)*

Back Wall: The rear wall of the stage or stage setting.

Bad Laugh: An audience laughing at the wrong moment.

Balance: The position and movements of the actors, the design of the set, lighting and costumes all are in a well-proportioned relationship.

Balcony: Areas of seating in a theater above the stalls.

Balcony Front: The vertical front face of a balcony.

Balls: A deep and resonant vocal tone.

Ballyhoo: Moving a followspot beam in a figure-eight pattern.

Banana: Direction to enter or exit a scene right or left in a gently curving path.

Band: The cast. Or, musicians playing together.

Banda: A small group of instrumentalists who play either on the stage or backstage, not in the pit, often as part of a crowd.

Banger: A large trailer with multiple dressing rooms, as in double banger, triple banger, four banger, etc.

Banjo: A rail along where a curtain runs.

Bank: A group of lighting units or dimmers arranged in rows.

Bankable: A person who can get a project financed solely by having their name attached.

Banking: Doing extra hours of school work to be free when needed on the set.

Bar Bells: Bar bells are rung in the theater to warn the audience that the performance is about to start or continue following an intermission, usually at two minutes before the performance.

Barn Doors: An apparatus with adjustable flaps that attaches to the front of a lighting instrument, used to block or shape the beam.

Basecamp: Area set up close to the shooting locations with all trucks, trailers, makeup, wardrobe, equipment, etc.

Bastard Prompt Corner: When the prompt corner is stage right instead of the usual stage left. This may be for architectural reasons in a theater with no wing space stage left, or because the layout of set would obscure a view from stage left.

Bastard Side (BS): Slang terminology used to describe stage right when there is a bastard prompt corner. Stage left is then known as Opposite Bastard.

Bathos: Comedy, with sexual jokes, harsh language, etc. *(Also known as Blue or Blue Comedy or Blue Humor or Working Blue)*

Baton: A short stick that the conductor uses to lead the orchestra.

Beat: A pause of varying length in the scene, usually to emphasize an emotion or a thought. A unit of action in a scene; a scene is made up of a series of beats.

Beat Sheet: An abbreviated description of the main events in a screenplay or story.

Beauty Shot: The last shot on a television or multimedia show, which is used to run the credits, or one that emphasizes something's attractive aspects.

Bed: The soundtrack that goes under a voiceover, such as music or sound effects.

Beef: A complaint from a patron or others concerning anything about the show.

Bee Smoker: A device that creates puffs of smoke to give the scene a smoke-filled look.

Beginners: Members of the cast who are on stage when the curtain goes up.

Bell: A signal that a take is ready to be made.

Below: Toward downstage.

Below the Line: There is an imaginary line on the first page of a film budget, separating the artistic elements of the budget from the technical elements. The artistic elements (writer, producer, director, actors) are listed above that line and the technical elements (crew, equipment costs, etc.) are listed below it.

Belt: A style of loud and full tone singing in musical theater productions.

Best Boy, Best Girl: Supervises the lighting and electrical equipment and serves as the right hand person of the Key Grip or Gaffer. *(Also known as First Assistant Electrician)*

Best Eight Bars: In a musical audition, an excerpted section of a song (typically 8 measures more or less) that displays the best of an actor's singing voice.

Between Engagements: Unemployed as an actor.

b.g., Bg, BG: Abbreviation for Background.

Bible: A document used for a television or multimedia show that contains important information about the show's characters, settings, and other elements.

Big: Actors giving too much of a performance in the interpretation of their scene, in terms of expression, voice levels, and body movement.

Big Close-Up (BCU): The closest face shot, showing from above the eyes to below the chin only. *(Also known as Big Head Close Up)*

Big Eyes: When the actor is instructed to open their eyes wide, without blinking or looking away, until focus is set for a big close up shot.

Big Four: Nickname for the four major commercial broadcast television networks in the United States, which are ABC, CBS, NBC, and Fox.

Big Head Close Up (BH/CU): The closest face shot, showing from above the eyes to below the chin only. *(Also known as Big Close Up)*

Bill: A playbill or program distributed at a theater.

Billboard: To emphasize or set apart a copy point is to billboard it.

Billboard Words: Words in a commercial that should be emphasized.

Billing: The list of names in the opening credits that usually reveals the size of an actor's role. The actor with the most time or is the biggest start usually gets top billing.

Biography (BIO): A short description of an actor's industry related experience or background.

Bird's-Eye View Shot: Taken from directly overhead and from a distance, often from on a crane or helicopter. *(Also known as Top Shot)*

Bite and Smile: Certain kinds of commercials, usually with food product where the actors do not speak.

Bit Part: A small part, usually consisting of a few lines.

Bit Player: A performer with a small speaking part.

Biz: Nickname for show business.

Black Box: When a theater room is surrounded in black curtains and the audience is in the same room with the performers.

Black Comedy: Morbid or grotesque themes and situations that could easily be tragic or horrifying if not treated with humor. *(Also known as Dark Comedy)*

Blackface: A face covered by black makeup, to represent a person of color, used extensively in minstrel shows from the 19th century well into the middle of the 20th century, but now understood to be offensive.

Black Out: An immediate shutdown of all stage lights.

Blacks: Black clothing worn by stage management during productions. Or, any black drapes or tabs, permanently or temporarily rigged, used for masking offstage areas. Blacks flown vertically at the edge of the stage are known as legs and those across the top of the stage are borders.

Blank: A gun cartridge with powder but no metal tip, allowing for the sound of a gunshot without a bullet.

Bleed: Blending or slurring between two phases of movement.

Bleed Through: Transformation from a scene downstage of a scrim to another scene upstage, by slowly crossfading lighting from downstage to upstage.

Blend: To smooth out makeup. Or, to dry-brush freshly painted scenery, so that two colors are irregularly smoothed together. Or, to adjust body movement, acting style, or vocal mannerisms to those of other actors for a more harmonious effect. Or, to adjust stage lighting to create even lighting as an actor passes from one stage area to another.

Blind Seat: A seat where a spectator can see only part of the stage.

Block: A wood or steel frame, with one or more pulleys to take fly lines. Or, a number of theater seats, taken together. Or, the director's work of positioning actors onstage and setting their entrances, exits, and other movement.

Block Booking: Selling a group of different films to theaters as a package, forcing theaters to take less desirable films in order to get the good ones.

Blocking: To set the movements of actors on a stage or set, which allows actors to avoid any awkward positions, such as one actor walking in front of another actor or standing with his or her back to the camera.

Blocking: In improv, rejecting information or ideas offered by another player. *(Also known as Denial)*

Blocking Rehearsal: The framework for the movement in a scene is recorded in the prompt book by the stage manager, assistant director, or even the director, then these notes are used to work with the actors early in the rehearsal period.

Blocking Stage: Rehearsing as if you were on a stage, but these early rehearsals are typically held in warehouses, parking lots or someone's living space.

Blocking Yourself: Getting behind furniture or other actors so that you cannot be seen by the audience.

Block Page: A script page that is all action description. Visually, the page is dense, with very little white space, and at looks like a block of paragraphs.

Blow: To forget one's lines or business.

Blue, Blue Comedy, Blue Humor: A style of performance, usually comedy, that is off-color, risqué, indecent or profane. *(Also known as Bathos or Working Blue)*

Blue Lights, Blues: Low wattage blue lights used to illuminate offstage obstacles and props tables, etc.

Blue Screen: A blank screen which acts as the backdrop to live action. Any background can be laid into the background and give the impression that the live action was really happening in the context of the blue screen.

B-Movie: A low budget movie that has a limited release or goes straight to video.

Board: The arrangement of scenes in the order to shoot.

the Board: The board posted at casting sessions that instructs the performer what to do and provides all the audition information.

Boards: A slang term for the stage floor — from the wood plank floor.

Body Double: Someone whose body is used in a movie or show instead of the body of the real actor.

Body Language: Communication that uses gestures, posture, and facial expressions instead of words.

BOH: *See Back of House.*

Bollywood: Nickname for the large film industry of India, centered in Bombay/Mumbai.

Book: A copy of the script, kept by the stage manager, which includes all cues and notes. Or, the spoken lines in a musical, as distinguished from the music and lyrics.

Booker: An agency employee who sets appointments for talent.

Book Flat: Two flats hinged together on the vertical edge that are free standing and normally used as a backing for a doorway or window.

Booking: A confirmed role for an actor.

Booking Agent: One who finds employment for artists from buyers of talent.

Booking Slip: A memorandum briefly outlining a performer's length of employment, payment amount, how the performer will be billed in the credits, and the start date.

Book Out: A call to an agent to let them know you are working, traveling or are unavailable for auditions or a job.

Book Show: A musical with a plot or storyline, as opposed to a revue.

Boom, Boom Mic: A microphone at the end of a long pole used over performers' heads to record their voices while keeping it out of the shot.

Boom Operator: Assistant to the production sound mixer, responsible for microphone placement, usually using a boom pole with a boom mic.

Boom Pole: A microphone stand that cannot stand on its own, used to reach the actor, out of view of the camera. *(Also known as a Fishpole)*

Booth: The area in the theater with the light and sound boards, usually in the back of the theater facing the stage.

Bootlegging: The unauthorized recording and selling of a performance of a song or movie.

Borders: The wide horizontal curtains or flats over the acting area that conceal the lights and other technical things overhead. *(Also known as Teasers)*

Bottom Lighting: The type of lighting that spiritualizes the subject.

Bounce: The fast in/out movement of the flown house curtain or drape, used during curtain calls. Or, the fast blackout/lights-up cues during curtain calls.

Bow: Response to positive attention received for a performance.

Box: A seating area in a theater, usually with 2-12 loose instead of fixed chairs, and separated from adjacent areas by railings or half walls. *(Also known as Opera Box)*

Box Boom: A mounting position, usually a vertical pipe, for stage spotlights at the front side of the auditorium.

Box Office: A place where tickets to a production are sold. Or, the commercial success of any production/performer based on profits and audience size.

Box Office Manager: A person in charge of ticketing and reservations.

Box Set: Naturalistic setting of a complete room built from flats with only the fourth wall missing.

Brace Weight: Cast iron weight placed to prevent movement of props. *(Also known as Pig Iron or Stage Weight)*

Brads: Brass fasteners used to bind a script printed on three-hole paper.

Brail: A rope, wire or chain attached at either end of a piece of scenery or lighting bar pulling it upstage or downstage of its naturally hanging position to allow another flying item to pass.

Bravo: A shouted word of applause, meaning excellent.

Break a Leg: A term used among actors before a performance or audition which means good luck.

Breakaway: Specially designed prop or set piece that looks solid but shatters easily.

Break Character: Stepping outside of the imaginary world of performance or out of the scene which you are doing.

Breakdown: Production's description by casting directors passed on to talent agents to find performers who fit the project.

Breaking In: A performer not waiting for their cue before they say or do something.

Breaking the Routine: In improv, interrupting an action with another action in order to advance the scene.

Breaking-Up: Out-of-place laughter by an actor on stage or during filming.

Brechtian Acting: An acting style where the actors purposely try to alienate the audience from the characters to constantly remind them they are watching a play, based on the theories of Bertolt Brecht. *(Also known as Anti-Naturalism)*

B-Reel: A cutaway to the actual scene, commonly used in news reporting, but also used in movies for flashback or simultaneous scenes. *(Also known as B-Roll)*

Bridge: A walkway, giving access to technical and service areas above the stage or auditorium, or linking fly-floors.

Bridging Shot: A shot used to cover a jump in time or place, or other discontinuity, such as falling calendar pages or seasons changing.

Brightness: Used by a director to tell an actor to exhibit more sparkle and personality.

Bright White Flash To: Whiteness will fill the screen for a brief moment as the show passes into the next scene.

Bring Up the Lights: To increase the illumination, usually of the entire theater.

Broad: An exaggerated performance.

Broadway: A major thoroughfare in New York City's midtown Manhattan Times Square area where many large theaters are located. It is the most famous theatrical district in the world.

Brokers: Agents.

B-Roll: A cutaway to the actual scene, commonly used in news reporting, but also used in movies for flashback or simultaneous scenes. *(Also known as B-Reel)*

Bromance: Slang for a buddy film, with an almost entirely male cast.

Brush Camera: Direction to an actor to exit a scene by walking directly at the camera and then brushing past it.

Bubble Show: A television or multimedia series that is nearing the end of the season and its future is uncertain.

Buddy Bar: Slang for a bar that works by friction against the ropes to let a piece in or out. *(Also known as Uncle Buddy)*

Build: Several beats combined resulting in heightened emotion or tension.

Building a Scene: Using dramatic devices, such as increased tempo, volume, and emphasis, to bring a scene to climax.

Bulldozing: Moving through a scene without paying attention to the other actors' offers and to push only your own ideas into the scene.

Bullet: Slang for a clothespin used as props or to hang props. *(Also known as 47 or Ammo or C-47 or CP47 or Peg)*

Bump: A one time payment for additional services. Or, to change the intensity of lighting instruments instantaneously, usually for a short duration of time, and often to the beat of music as if to create a pulsing effect.

Bump Up: An upgrade in pay and billing when an extra says a few words or other special activity in a scene. Or, to turn up the lights.

Burlesque: Any comic entertainment or revue sketch that pokes fun at current manners, many times featuring women in scant costumes.

Bus-and-Truck Tour: A low-budget tour of a play or musical, usually presented in smaller cities for a very short run.

Business: Any specific action or gestures, other than crossing, performed on the stage, such as picking up a book or turning on a television set.

the Business: Slang for show business.

Business Manager: Handles the financial affairs of the artist and may work for a large management firm with several clients, or as a dedicated partner to one group or individual. This person may also be the publicist, booking agent, and personal manager if the client does not have a full team.

Buskin: The thick-soled, laced, leather boot worn by actors in Greek tragedy to give them added height, and, thereby perceived dignity. *(Also known as Cothurnus)*

Button: A joke on a sitcom that ends a scene. Or, a final picture usually before a blackout or fadeout.

Buyout: A one-time payment for shooting and airing a commercial, meaning a flat fee with no residuals.

C

C: Abbreviation for Centerstage, to identify the center of the stage. *(See Appendix: STAGE DIRECTION ABBREVIATIONS)*

C-47: Slang for a clothespin used as props or to hang props. *(Also known as 47 or Ammo or Bullet or CP47 or Peg)*

C-74: A pair of wooden tweezers made from flipping the spring on a clothespin.

Cabaret: Entertainment held in a nightclub or restaurant while the audience eats or drinks at tables.

Cable: Refers to something that will only run only on cable channels.

Call: The time that an actor or crew member must report to the set. *(Also known as Call Time)*

Callback: A second or subsequent round of auditions for the same role, which may include the producer and director, or in the case of commercials, is usually filmed for final consideration.

Call Back: Bringing back an idea from earlier in the scene, or from a previous scene in the show, or even from a previous performance. *(Also known as Reincorporation)*

Call Board: The place backstage where the stage manager puts up important information for the cast and crew.

Calling Service: For extras, a company that helps to book them on jobs.

Calling the Show: The process of giving verbal cues to the lighting, sound, fly operators and stage crew during the performance, usually done from the prompt corner by the stage manager or ASM over cans.

Call Sheet: The daily sheet for a production that lists all the scenes to be shot that day as well as actor and crew arrival times.

Call Time: The time which someone has to be on the set. *(Also known as Call)*

Call Time Pulled: Call time is earlier than originally scheduled.

Call Time Pushed: Call time is later than originally scheduled.

Cameo: A very small part in a film, usually done by a well-known actor.

Camera Blocking: Giving the camera operators their movement and framing instructions.

Camera Crew: A team in charge of everything to do with the cameras.

Camera Left (CL): Indicates the side of the shot where the performers are kept from the camera operator's perspective. *(Also known as Left Frame)*

Camera Operator: The person responsible for operation of the camera and looking through the lens during a take during the physical filming and often works under the cinematographer. *(Also known as Second Cameraman)*

Camera Ready: Description of anyone who is completely ready to appear on camera in full dress and makeup.

Camera Rehearsal: To perform a role at less than usual intensity, such as during a technical rehearsal. *(Also known as Walk Through)*

Camera Right (CR): Indicates the side of the shot where the performers are kept, from the camera operator's perspective. *(Also known as Right Frame)*

Camera Shots: The amount of space seen in one shot or frame, used to show different aspects of characters, settings, and themes, broken down into three main shot sizes: Long/ Wide, Medium, and Close. *(See Appendix: CAMERA SHOTS)*

Canadian Cross: When an actor crosses the scene, without actually taking the focus in the story, as to add something to the scene. For instance, for a scene in a campground, an actor crosses the scene being chased by a swarm of mosquitoes.

Cans: Slang term for headphones.

Cap: Performer completing their section of the scene.

Capacity: The total number of seats available for the audience.

Carnival Mass: A type of work originally designed to be performed on Shrove Tuesday, the last day before Lent begins. The play uses elements of Catholic liturgy, social morality, music from the Catholic Mass, masks, puppets, and characters such as the wise-fool. Dating from the 15th century and found in many Christian cultures.

Carpenter: A person who works on the construction of the sets.

Carry: To be the acting mainstay of a production.

Cashew: Shorter than a Banana, direction to an actor to enter or exit a scene right or left in a gently curving path.

Cast: The group of actors performing in a particular production. Or, the final status of an actor that has won a role or part in a production over other competing performers.

Cast Contingent, Cast Contingency: When an entity orders a pilot with the caveat that production can't start until a there has been a suitable, usually well-known actor cast in the starring role.

Casting: When a casting director puts out the news that they need to fill a certain role that requires an approximate age range and appearance such as a certain ethnicity, height, build or look. Or, the process of actors being cast for the role, done by the casting director and/or the director or producer.

Casting Agent: A person who finds actors for a production.

Casting Breakdown: A synopsis of the film and short description of each character that are cast (e.g., gender, age, race, etc.). This may also include audition days, location and tentative shoot dates.

Casting Director (CD): The person responsible for casting.

Casting Facility: A studio or office space used by one or more casting directors to hold auditions.

Casting Notice: Similar to casting breakdown, except this one is available to the public and is often listed on casting websites.

Casting Office: A company that makes available suitable actors for a producer.

Casting Society of America (CSA): A professional organization of casting directors working in theater, film, television, and multimedia. CSA is not a union or a guild, therefore every casting director working is not necessarily a member of this organization. *(See Appendix: ENTERTAINMENT INDUSTRY ASSOCIATIONS/ORGANIZATIONS)*

Cast List: A list of actors and their roles.

Cast Page: A page that typically follows the title page of a script, listing the characters, with very brief descriptions of each.

Casuals: Part-time temporary technicians paid by the hour.

Catalog: All the songs owned by a music publisher considered as one collection.

Catcall: A sound of disapproval, usually from the audience.

Caterer: The person responsible for all the food on the set or stage.

Catharsis: The feeling of release at the end of a tragedy experienced by audience members who have undergone feelings of fear and pity, shared in the troubles of the play's protagonist, and now are set free from the emotional grip of the action. Aristotle called this cleansing the pleasure of tragedy. *(Also known as Katharsis)*

Cattle Call: Auditions that are open to all types of actors: professionals, amateurs, union, and non-union members.

Catwalk: A very narrow walkway on the ceiling of a theater from which lights and scenery are hung.

CD: *See Casting Director.*

Ceiling: A flat, in one piece, or hinged in two or more pieces, or a cloth or drape, hung horizontally to form the top of an interior set, concealing the flies.

Celebrity: Famous individuals or anyone who has had any moderate public attention in media, regardless of how well-known they are beyond their niche.

Censor: To cause a dramatic piece or production to be suppressed or altered by governmental action, when it does not conform to legal requirements, usually for nudity or obscenity. Or, the name of a government official charged with this responsibility.

Censorship: A governmental action where a play or production is altered or even banned because it violates certain statutes, such as for nudity or language.

Center: The part of the body chosen to dominate movement.

Center Line (CL): Imaginary line running down the stage through the exact center of the proscenium opening, marked as CL on stage plans. Normally marked on the stage floor or rehearsal room and used as a reference when marking out or assembling a set.

Center of Interest: The point in the production where the attention of the audience is meant to rest, shifting with the movements of the actors, lighting, or other reasons.

Center Stage: The central part of a theatrical stage.

Central Conflict: The oppositional force between characters that directly affects or motivates the action of the plot.

CGI: *See Computer Generated Imagery.*

Change Motion: When a discovery of some kind takes place within a scene or monologue that drastically changes the direction of that scene or monologue.

Change Music: The music played between scenes while sets are being changed.

Changes: Different outfits worn by a performer during a production.

Channel: A spot on the electromagnetic spectrum that the FCC licenses to a specific station.

Chaperone: An adult who takes responsibility for a group of young people while they're on set.

Character: The person who is going to be played by an actor during a production.

Character Actor: An actor or actress who specializes in playing secondary roles. These parts are not the romantic lead, but the additional funny, scary, or otherwise exaggerated roles.

Character Analysis: The written biography of a character. *(Also known as Character Sketch)*

Character Arc: The emotional progress of the characters.

Character Core: The character's core personality helps to define who he/she/it is, which should be an interested and flawed being.

Character Description: A few lines of powerful character details in a script when a new character is introduced, so the description will grab the attention of the reader as well as potential actors.

Character Development: The character's looks, background, history, personality, psychology, and current goals.

Characterization: The actor using their craft to explore and develop the specific qualities of a character.

Character Model: A model who, while not necessarily a classic beauty, has strong or interesting facial features and selling attributes for specific products.

Character Part: A role where an actor portrays traits that differ from his or her own to produce a desired character.

Character Role: A supporting role with pronounced or eccentric characteristics.

Character Sketch: The written biography of a character. *(Also known as Character Analysis)*

Charts: Musical arrangements.

Chase: Repeated sequence of changing lighting that gives the effect of the moving lights.

Cheat: An actor movement or lighting change that happens without the audience being aware of it. Or, an angle where an actor is being positioned that will better accommodate the camera.

Cheat a Script: Adjusting the margins and spacing of a screenplay on a page to fool the reader into thinking the script is shorter.

Cheating: Angling or squaring the body out toward the audience or camera, while still partly facing the other character. *(Also known as Opening Out)*

Cheating Shots: When lights, actors or other elements are adjusted after they've already been shot in order to create a better shot.

Cheat Out: Technique of pivoting the torso so that the face is toward the audience even when the actor's body is facing sideways.

Check: To assess the sound in the venue. Or, to lower the brightness of a light to zero.

Checking the Gate: After a scene has been shot, the camera assistant checks the lens to make sure there was nothing in the mechanism of the camera which could ruin the film.

Chewing the Scenery: To overact, especially in emotional scenes.

Chick Flick: Slang for films with heavy emotion and usually strong female characters.

Chief Electrician: A person in charge of an electrical team. *(Also known as Gaffer or Head Electrician or Key Electrician)*

Children's Theater: A theater specializing in entertainment for children.

Chivalry: Not clinging to your own ideas as a character.

Chocker, Chocker Close Up (CH/SH): A shot that frames the actor's face from just below the mouth to just above the eyebrows.

Chord: Three or more notes sounded simultaneously that imply a harmonic function.

Choregus: Title given to a wealthy citizen in ancient Greece who was selected to pay for the training and costumes of the chorus in dramas.

Choreographer: A person responsible for arranging movements and creating dances for actors to perform.

Choreography: The dances that are designed for a production.

Chorus: A group of performers who sing, dance, or recite together in a production. Or, the chorus is the section of the song that repeats itself at certain intervals. At the turn of the century, and continuing into the sixties, choruses were compared and shaped within thirty-two bars of music.

Chronicle Play: A play with a historical basis, told as a series of episodes rather than as a complete story with a structured plot. Shakespeare's Richard II, based on Raphael Holinshed's Chronicles is an example.

Cinema: Building where acting or the showing of a movie takes place. Or, the production of movies as an art or industry.

Cinemascope: An optical system that has different magnifications in the vertical and horizontal dimensions of the picture.

Cinematographer: The expert responsible for capturing, recording or photographing images for a film, through the selection of visual recording devices, camera angles, film stock, lenses, framing, and arrangement of lighting. *(Also known as Cinematographer or First Cameraman or Director of Photography)*

Cinema Verite: The documentary style of film which gained popularity in the 50's and literally means camera truth.

Circle: The balcony with tiered seating above the stalls. *(Also known as Grand Circle)*

Circle of Intention: The extent or range of concentration.

Circle Takes: A director's favorite or most usable filming of a particular scene, used to expedite the editing process.

Citizen Kane: Revered by most in the entertainment industry as the most important American film (1941) ever made. The timeless masterpiece was co-written, directed, and produced by Orson Welles (1915-1985), who also played the lead. It is a mystery, a character study, a drama, a political thriller, a romance, a tragedy, etc.

CL: The center line on stage plans. Or, camera left in filming. Or, the center left of a Proscenium stage, from the actor's point of view.

Clapboard, Clapper, Clapperboard: The board which is photographed at the start of each take to identify the shot and to establish sound synchronization by the clapping of a stick. The clapboard is the combination of the chalkboard slate that holds information identifying the next scene and the clapstick which is used to align sound and picture. It is used in filmmaking and video production to assist in the synchronizing of picture and sound, and to designate and mark particular scenes recorded during a production. The noise the clapper makes is identified on the audio track, and the shutting of the clapstick is identified on the visual track. The two tracks can then be precisely synchronized. Other nicknames include Clacker, Slapperboard, Sync Slate, Time Slate, Sticks, Board, Smart Slate, Dumb Slate, and Sound Marker. *(Also known as Slate or Slate Board)*

Clapstick: The bar that is raised and lowered on the clapboard which creates the noise that can be identified easily on the audio track.

Claptrap: Any exaggerated or artificial gesture, rhetorical delivery, or content.

Claque: A group of people hired to lead the applause. *(Also known as Klak)*

Class A Network Spot: Commercial airing at prime time on a major network for which residuals are highest.

Classic Acting: An acting style marked by restraint and formality in the depiction of passion, by polished, stately movement, gesture, and delivery.

Classic Drama: Any play written before the present century. Actors auditioning are often asked to prepare two monologues, one classical and one modern.

Clean Entrance: In film, this is a direction to an actor to be all the way out of a shot and walk into it.

Cleaners: Auditorium lights used for cleaning and setting up the auditorium before the house lights are switched on.

Clean Exit: In film, this is a direction to an actor to exit all the way out of a frame.

Clear: Indication to a performer to get out of the way of another actor. Or, to get off the set when a rehearsal or scene is about to begin. Or, when a crew member indicates that a particular flying piece is safe to fly, or a particular item of scenery has passed a danger point.

Clearance: Message passed to stage management from the front of house manager that the house is ready for the performance to begin.

Clearance Agency: Performance rights organizations, such as ASCAP, BMI, and SESAC, which license and collect royalties for performance of its members of songwriters, composers and music publishers.

Clearing Stick: A long rod used to rescue flying objects or to prevent them from becoming entangled by guiding flying scenery past obstructions.

Clear Yourself: A performer making sure they are in clear view of the camera.

Clicks: The number of frames shown per beat.

Clicks and Pops: A dry mouth produces much more mouth noise than a damp one. The less mouth noise, the less editing has to be done later. *(Also known as Mouth Noise)*

Click Track: A perforated sound track that produces click sounds that enables people a predetermined beat in synchronization with the movie.

Climatic Form: A series of dramatic incidents with a direct causal link.

Climax: The turning point in a plot or dramatic action, and is the highest moment of conflict.

Clip: A brief segment excerpted from a film.

Close: To conclude or end a production. Or, to perform in the last number on a program.

Closed Set: A time when only a few authorized people are allowed on the set, which means there is a probably a nude scene or love scene being filmed.

Close-Up (CU): A close shot that fills the screen with part of the actor, such as the actor's face or head.

Closing Off: An actor's action of turning away from the audience, the opposite of opening up.

Cloth: Backdrop scenery painted on fabric, usually hung from a banjo.

Cold, Cold Open: A technique of jumping directly into a story at the beginning or opening of a show before the title sequence or opening credits are shown. *(Also known as Teaser)*

Cold Read, Cold Reading: An audition where the actor is asked to read from copy they are not familiar with, generally with little or no time to prepare.

Co-Lead: Characters who are equally important to the storyline of a given project.

Collaboration: Two or more people working together in a joint intellectual effort.

Collaborator: One of two or more partners in an artistic project.

Color-Blind Casting: When characters for a performed work are cast without regard to race, gender, age, etc., or cast against what is specified. (i.e., an adult plays a child, an African American actor plays a part previously only played by Caucasian actors, a woman plays a previously male role, etc.). *(Also known as Non-Traditional Casting)*

Color Composition: The term for colors in a shot or a frame.

Color Cover: A stand-in wearing the same color as the principal actor.

Colored Pages: Pages where script rewrites are copied.

Color Scheme: The term for colors in the whole film.

Combo: A small group of instrumentalists.

Comedian: A person known professionally for telling funny jokes.

Come Down: Signifies the end of a show, when the curtain, if there is one, comes down.

Comedy: A theatrical work that is intentionally humorous.

Comedy of Errors: Usually features a series of interconnected misunderstandings.

Comic Opera: A humorous or satirical operetta.

Comic Relief: A comic or farcical scene or incident introduced into tragedy or any serious play to give the audience a momentary respite from emotional tension before further tension is required.

Commedia dell'arte: A professional form of theatrical improvisation, developed in Italy in the 1500s, featuring stock characters and standardized plots.

Commentator: A voice commenting on the action of a film, but unlike a narrator, provides supposedly unbiased information, maintaining apparent perspective and distance from what occurs on the screen.

Commenting: Stepping out of the reality of the scene by saying or doing something that refers to the fact that it's a scene being played. *(Also known as Stepping Out)*

Commercial: Regarding the industry, the potential to sell, or that which has mass appeal. Or, a television, multimedia, or radio advertisement.

Commission: Percentage of income paid by actors to their representative. If it is an agent, the amount cannot be over 10% for a union contract, but if it is a manager, the percentage is unregulated, though is traditionally 15-20%.

Common-Law Copyright: Natural protection of a song based on common laws of the various states, superseded by a single national system effective January 1, 1978.

Community Theater: A local theater group in a city or town.

Comp: Short for complimentary or free ticket.

Company: The whole cast and crew of a production.

Company Manager: The person in charge of a touring cast when they are traveling to different performance locations. *(Also known as Road Manager)*

Comp Card: A type of head shot that positions 3-5 different images of the subject together on one 8 x 10 spread giving casting directors a quick way to determine how the subject will look in different settings, and may include bio and contact information. *(Also known as Composite or Composite Card)*

Completed: For a movie, there is a final print, but it has not yet been screened.

Complication: The second act of a three-act dramatic structure, where the plot takes a dramatic turn.

Complimentary: A seat or ticket that is provided free, as to a reviewer, parents of a cast member, a contributor or other supporter, etc.

Composer: One who writes the music to a song.

Composite, Composite Card: A type of head shot popular in the commercial industry which positions 3-5 different images of the subject together on one 8 x 10 spread giving casting directors a quick way to determine how the subject will look in different settings, and many times includes bio and contact information. *(Also known as Comp Card)*

Composition: The arrangement of the staging and design elements to create a visual picture. Or, the art of writing music or the musical work itself.

Comps: Free tickets. Actors are usually given comps to offer to their friends, agents, and casting directors for their performances.

Compulsory License: Statutory mandate given to a copyright owner to permit third parties to make sound recordings of the copyright owner's song after it has been recorded.

Computer Generated Imagery (CGI): The application of computer graphics to create or contribute to images in films, television, multimedia, etc.

Concentration: The ability of the actor to be in character in dialog, attitude, etc.

Concept Meeting: A gathering of the producer, director and casting director to reach an agreement about the look and quality of each character in a script.

Concept Musical: A series of loosely connected scenes that focus on a theatrical concept.

Concession: A merchandising stand in the foyer of the theater.

Concessionaire: A person who buys the right to operate a refreshment stand or similar business supported by the purchases of theater patrons.

Conclusion: The result of conflict and completion of premise.

Conductor: The leader of the orchestra. *(Also known as Maestro)*

Confidant, Confidante: The role of a close friend of a principal character, used dramatically for purposes of exposition, characterization, or development of dramatic action. The lead character can thus express ideas, explain feelings, or outline plans of action in a very natural way.

Conflict: An essential and vital element of acting that involves the obstacles and struggles, both inner and outer, that a character must overcome.

Conflicts: Being under contract for two conflicting productions.

Console: The control panel that allows the engineer to direct the audio signal to the recorders, and to combine the various audio components into the final mix.

Consumer Publication: Entertainment oriented periodicals written and published for a general public readership, such as Rolling Stone, etc.

Contact Sheet: A list of names and contact details (e.g., phone numbers, addresses, etc.) for the cast and crew. Or, a sheet showing all of the frames from a roll of film to enable a choice to be made about which to enlarge properly.

Context: Interrelated conditions where a play exists or occurs, as in the broader setting for the scene (e.g., political, social, etc).

Continuity: Matching action in each take of a scene with the same props, dialogue, extras, wardrobe, make up, etc.

CONTINUOUS: Sometimes, instead of DAY or NIGHT at the end of a Slugline/location description, you'll see CONTINUOUS, which refers to action that moves from one location to another location without any interruptions in time.

Continuous Action: Stated in the script as CONTINUOUS, and included in the scene heading when moving from one scene to another as the action continues.

Continuous Shot Feature Film: A full-length movie filmed in one long take by a single camera, or manufactured to give the impression it was. *(Also known as One-Shot Feature Film)*

Contract: To secure the rights to perform a work, a theater company must sign a binding legal document where the company agrees to all stipulations. Or, the document an actor signs when accepting a role.

Contrast: Diversity, variation, used to heighten interest, such as dramatic construction, acting, lighting, set design, etc.

Contra-Zoom: An unsettling camera special effect that appears to undermine normal visual perception. A stationary object is filmed as the camera moves towards or away from it while adjusting its focal point so that the object remains the same size relative to the rest of the scene, accomplished by pulling the camera away from the focal object while zooming in at the same rate. *(Also known as Dolly Zoom or Hitchcock Zoom or Vertigo Effect)*

Contrived: Portrayal of a character or ending, etc., which is arranged by a dramatist, without concern for plausibility.

Control Booth, Control Room: A glass-enclosed area full of equipment where an engineer and director sit during dubbing sessions. Or, a small room or place in the theater where all technical things, lights and sound, are controlled.

Conventions: Alternative ways of presenting parts of a drama.

Conversation Piece: A play that emphasizes dialogue rather than action or movement.

Coogan Law: Refers to landmark legislation in the late 1930s designed to protect a child actor's earnings, by depositing some of the minor's earnings in a court administered trust fund that the child receives when they reach the age of maturity, named after child actor Jackie Coogan (1914-1984).

Coordinates: Costumes that are separates, which are interchangeable, or sometimes reversible, such as ties, vests, and so on.

Co-Publishing: The joint publication of one copyrighted work by two publishers.

Copy: A slang term for dialogue or script.

Copy Points: The items in a script that require particular attention, and therefore particular interpretation by the actor.

Copyright: The exclusive rights granted to authors and composers for protection of their work. Or, to secure protection for a piece of work by filling the proper registration forms with the Copyright Office.

Copyright Infringement: Stealing or using somebody else's copyrighted work.

Copyright Notice: A notice comprised of three elements: the symbol of copyright or the word copyright or both, the year the work has been registered for copyright or the year the work was completed, and the copyright owner's name.

Copyright Office: Federal government department whose main purpose is to file and supply information regarding copyrights.

Copywriter: A person who creates the text of advertisements or publicity material.

Corner: The place from which the stage manager controls the show. *(Also known as Prompt Corner)*

Corner Plate: A triangle of plywood used to strengthen the corners of a flat.

Corpse, Corpsing: An actor who gets an unintended and uncontrollable fit of laughter on stage.

Costar: The other actors who have main parts.

Costume: Clothing worn by an actor during a performance.

Costume Designer: The individual who designs the actors' clothing.

Costume Fitting: Getting fitted for a costume by the costume designer or assistant. The actor is usually measured early in the rehearsal process and fitted with the costume later.

Costume Parade: The actors will all model their costumes for the director to approve or discuss changes with the costume designer.

Costume Plot: A list of characters, showing the costumes to be worn in a production, scene by scene.

Costumer: The person responsible for costumes.

Costume Shop: A special area set aside for the making of the costumes or for adjusting those that are rented.

Cothurnus: The thick-soled, laced, leather boot worn by actors in Greek tragedy to give them added height, and, thereby perceived dignity. *(Also known as Buskin)*

Countercross: The movement, in opposite directions, by two or more actors to balance the stage picture.

Countering: A blocking movement by an actor to rebalance the stage in reaction to another actor's movement, or change of position.

Counter Rake: Modifying furniture or props by shortening the upstage legs, etc., so that they can stand level on a raked stage.

Count the House: The number of seats sold. Or, to stare at the audience while acting.

Coup de Theater: A theatrical success. Or, a sudden and unforeseen, but not necessarily illogical turn of events in the course of a play.

Courier 12: The only universally acceptable font and size of font for scripts.

Cove: Front of house catwalk lighting positions.

Cover: Another term for understudy. Or, the use of ad-lib to hide from the audience any kind of mistake. Or, another artist's version of a song already recorded.

Coverage: The closer shots taken in a scene to be inserted in to the master.

Covering: To make up dialogue and or blocking due to a mistake or accident onstage without breaking character.

Cover Set: A set which is always ready for shooting on a moment's notice.

Cover Shot: An additional shot that might be of a different angle to a master shot, done for editing purposes.

Cowboy: Getting its name from the westerns of the 1930-40s to show the actor's gun holsters, this shot frames from mid-thighs up. Tight cowboy means above guns. *(Also known as American)*

Co-Writing: Joint authorship of one work by two or more writers.

CP47: Slang for a clothespin used as props or to hang props. *(Also known as 47 or Ammo or Bullet or C-47 or Peg)*

Craft, Craft Services: The table on a set, with food and snacks for the cast and crew. Or, the company or department that provides food service and beverages to the other departments on the set.

Crane Shot: A shot of a scene from above, often with the camera hanging on a crane.

Crash Box: Sealed metal box filled with broken plates, dishes, cups, and other similar items, which can be dropped or thrown offstage to simulate breaking glass, plates, etc.

Crawl: Superimposed titles or text intended to move across/up/down/diagonally on screen. For example, the text at the beginning of the movie Star Wars "crawls" up into infinity.

Creative Drama: An improvisational, process-centered form of theater where participants are guided by a leader to imagine, enact, and reflect on human experiences.

Creative Fee: What you are paid if you are asked to do improv for an audition.

Credits: Appearance at the beginning or end of a film or show of names involved in the production. Or, the list of and actor's experience on their resume.

Crepe Hair: Artificial hair that can be cut and trimmed to form eyebrows, mustaches and beards.

Crew: Everyone on the set who is contributing to the production, except for the cast.

Crew Call: The time the crew is expected to be on set.

Crew Chief, Crew Head: The chief of the stage staff, in charge of building and shifting scenery.

Crisis: A decisive point in the plot of a play where the outcome of the remaining action depends.

Critique: Opinions and comments based on predetermined criteria that may be used for self-evaluation or the evaluation of the actors or the production itself.

Cross: A move by an actor from one position to another.

Cross Collateralization: Recouping the money spent on one piece of work against the earnings of another one.

Cross Cutting: The film technique which cuts between two scenes in order to show action taking place in consecutively, or even simultaneously.

Crossfade: To change from one lighting cue to another with no blackout in between, or to change from one sound cue to another with no silence in between.

Crossing: To move from one point on the stage to another, especially to a diametrically opposed point.

Crosslight: To illuminate the stage with two crossing beams of light.

Crossover: A song which receives airplay in more than one market.

Crowd Shot: Shows a large group of people, however CGI is now often used to film very large crowd shots to avoid huge costs associated with hiring extras. *(Also known as a Group Shot)*

CS: Abbreviation for Centerstage, to identify the center of the stage. *(See Appendix: STAGE DIRECTION ABBREVIATIONS)*

CSA: *See Casting Society of America.*

Cue: The action, line, or phrase of dialogue that signals a character to move or speak. Or, another term for the talk back system in a recording studio conducted through headphones.

Cue Cards: The large flash cards that have an actor's script printed on them. *(Also known as Idiot Cards)*

Cue Light: System for giving technical staff silent cues by light. Red light means stand-by or warn, green light means go. Ensures greater precision when visibility or audibility of actors is limited. Sometimes used for cueing actors to the set.

Cue-to-Cue: A rehearsal where to save time, action and text is cut out between cues.

Curriculum Vitae: Short account of one's career or qualifications as in a resume.

Curtain: A screen of cloth on stage that separates the audience from the performers.

Curtain Call: The time at the end of a stage performance when all the actors take their bows. *(Also known as Walkdown)*

Curtain Line: The imaginary line across the stage floor which follows the line of the front curtain.

Curtain Music: Music played just before the beginning or resumption of an act.

Curtain Speech: A speech, usually given at the end of a performance that is a short acknowledgment or announcement delivered in front of the closed main drape by the author, manager, or an actor.

Curtain Time: The time a performance is scheduled to begin.

Curtain Up: The start of a performance, whether or not an actual curtain exists in front of the stage.

Curtain Warmer: Soft light projected onto the grand drape or main curtain when the audience is being seated.

Cut: The director's cue to stop filming. Or, to omit lines or business provided in the script, usually intentionally. Or, to make or be a recorded selection.

Cut and Hold: Direction to stop the action and hold positions. Sometimes means that this is the final take for this scene and that the camera operator is checking the gate to be certain that the film is in the can to call a wrap.

Cutaway: A shot of something specific, other than the actors, and away from the main scene.

Cut Drop: A drop, painted and then cut out so that the spectator sees a scene formed not only by the drop, but also by whatever is placed behind it.

Cut In: To break into the speech of another character. Or, a shot similar to a cutaway, but shows a close-up shot of something visible in the main scene.

Cut Off Lines: Lines interrupted by another speaker and indicated by dashes in the script.

Cut Out: A free-standing piece of scenery, such as a tree, cut out of board into the correct shape and painted.

Cuts: Lines, speeches, songs, or any other element in a printed script left out of a particular production.

Cutting: The process where strips of film are cut and joined together. *(Also known as Editing)*

Cutting Room, Cutting Room Floor: The phrase used when films are edited and portions taken out that therefore end up on the "Cutting Room Floor." *(Also known as On the Floor)*

CUT TO: The most simple and common transition in a script that describes a change of scene over the course of one frame.

Cut Version: A script with dialogue deleted.

Cyc, Cyclorama: Pronounced Sike, the Cyc is a curved plain cloth or plastered wall filling the rear of the stage or television, or multimedia studio.

D

D: Abbreviation for Downstage. *(See Appendix: STAGE DIRECTION ABBREVIATIONS)*

Dailies: Raw footage shot that day and yet to be edited. *(Also known as Rushes)*

Daisy-Chaining: Connecting items of equipment together by linking from one to the next in a chain.

Dark: An evening where a theater is not scheduled to have a public performance. *(Also known as Dark Night)*

Dark Comedy: Morbid or grotesque themes and situations that could easily be tragic or horrifying if not treated with humor. *(Also known as Black Comedy)*

Dark Night: An evening where a theater is not scheduled to have a public performance. *(Also known as Dark)*

DAT: Abbreviation for Digital Audio Tape.

Date: A recording session or live engagement.

Day: Whenever the action of a story moves into a new period, it is a day. The script days are numbered consecutively, no matter how much time elapses between them.

Day For Night: A shot being filmed during the day, which appears on the screen to be a night scene.

Day-Out-of-Days (DOOD): Schedule made by the assistant director assigning time slots for when certain people or things will work on set.

Day Performer: The person hired to work on a production on a day-to-day basis, not on a contract.

Day Player: Someone who is hired at SAG-AFTRA scale (minimum) for the day.

Day Shot: A specific scene in the script to be filmed or taped while the sun is out.

DBO: *See Dead Blackout.*

DC: Abbreviation for Downstage Center. *(See Appendix: STAGE DIRECTION ABBREVIATIONS)*

Dead: Scenery or equipment not needed for current production. Or, a pre-plotted height for a piece of scenery or lighting bar, also known at trim.

Dead Air: A period of silence or an unintended interruption in between lines during which there is no sound.

Dead Blackout (DBO): A sudden, instantaneous switching off of all lights.

Dead Hang: A flat or curtain that hangs with the bottom edge level on the stage floor without a counterweight.

Deadpan: Line delivery with no expression in face or voice.

Deads: The positional indicators on the rope of a pre-plotted height for a piece of scenery or lighting bar.

Deal Memo: A document created between the producer, casting director and agent that describes the payment amount, method, and any rider stipulations.

Death at the Box Office: A dramatic piece or actor that is unlikely to succeed with the public or known to be unpopular.

Death Role: A character who dies.

Debut: An actor's first appearance, whether at the beginning of their career, or in a new theater. Or, the first performance or showing of a production.

Deck: Stage area.

Deep: A stage or acting area that is long in measurement from front to back.

Deep Focus: A degree of focus such that everything in frame is in focus.

Delay: A narrative and dramatic device used to strengthen the established tension. By delaying the arrival of an expected character or event, the solution of a mystery or an answer to an unanswered question, a more powerful impact is achieved on the audience.

Delivery: The manner where an actor presents or utters their lines.

Delivery Manager: The person responsible for supplying the physical elements for a production, including the legal elements such as copyright registration, rights documents insurance, copyright and title searches and talent agreements. *(Also known as Distribution Manager)*

Demo: Short for demonstration, this can be a sample tape of a talent's voice used to show his or her abilities.

Demo Firm: An organization specializing in the production of demo tapes.

Demo Reel: A short amount of footage that showcases a performer's skills. *(Also known as Short Reel)*

Denial: In improv, rejecting ideas by another player. *(Also known as Blocking)*

Denouement: The final resolution or clarification of a dramatic or narrative plot or the final outcome of a complex sequence of events.

Department: The principal divisions of the stage staff, headed by a company official, such as wardrobe, scenery, lighting, etc.

Depth of Field: The range of distance within focus.

Deputy Stage Manager (DSM): Assistant Stage Manager.

De-Rig: Removing lighting instruments and cabling from flying bars or grid to return the venue to its normal state, in preparation for the next production.

Descending Action: At the end of the second act, and the main culmination is reached, the descending action starts the third act with a new tension.

Design: The creative process of developing and executing aesthetic or functional designs in a production, such as costumes, lighting, sets, and makeup.

Designer: Designs all aspects of the production, except lighting, including the set, costumes, wigs, makeup, etc.

Desilu Productions: The first independent television production company, founded by Lucille Ball (1911-1989) and Desi Arnaz (1917-1986) to prove that they could make the sitcom "I Love Lucy" work, and used $5,000 of their own money to produce the pilot for the series, which made popular the use of the three-camera system for television.

Desk: A control desk, either for lighting or sound.

Deus Ex Machina: Means the god from the machine. In Greek classical drama, an actual machine lowered the actor playing the god into the center of the action so that he or she could unravel the plot complications and direct the denouement. Now the term denotes a play that uses a trick ending to extricate the actors from impossible situations.

Deuteragonist: The second character added to Greek classical drama. Previous to that, there were only a chorus and protagonist.

Development: The pre-approval stage with simply a writer with an idea or a producer with a concept.

DG: *See Dramatists Guild of America.*

DGA: *See Directors Guild of America.*

Dialect: A regional accent that is often adopted by actors to make the role more believable.

Dialect Coach: Assists an actor in assuming a certain regional accent in order to perform convincingly in radio, theatrical or film productions. Dialect coaches are skilled in diction and linguistics, and do not necessarily have to have the accent that they are teaching. *(See Dialogue Coach)*

Dialectical Theater: An acting style or form of theater based on the principle of using live performance as a means of social and political commentary. This started in the early 1920-30s characterized by the use of such artificial devices as cartoons, posters, and film sequences distancing the audience from theatrical illusion and following focus on the play's message. *(See Epic Theater or Theater of Alienation)*

Dialogue: The written words spoken by the actors.

Dialogue Coach: Assists an actor in assuming a certain regional accent in order to perform convincingly in radio, theatrical or film productions. Dialect coaches are skilled in diction and linguistics, and do not necessarily have to have the accent that they are teaching. *(See Dialect Coach)*

Dialogue Director: Reviews lines with actors to ensure memorization, interpretation and/or dialect.

Dialogue-less Commercials: Used to emphasize a visual image with the spoken words of an announcer as the only recorded sound.

Dialogue Replacement: The recording of dialogue to match previously recorded film or video.

Diaphragm: The lower part of the lungs, filling the abdominal space, that supports the voice when actors and singers breathe correctly on stage.

Dichroic Filter: Glass color filters which reflect all light except that which is the color of the filter, which passes through.

Dichroic Light: Low voltage display lamp with a reflector that lets heat pass through it, rather than reflecting it, resulting in a much cooler light.

Diction: Clear, sharp pronunciation of words, especially of consonants.

Die: When a production or performance fails to please the audience.

Diegetic: Sound that would logically be heard by characters in their current situation or locale.

Diffusing Medium: A translucent sheet of frosted plastic or gel, used to tone down lighting, or provide a soft light.

Digital Audio Tape: A signal recording and playback medium developed by Sony and introduced in 1987, which is digital rather than analog.

Digital Multiplex (DMX): A communications protocol used in stage lighting.

Dilemma: The opening problem.

Dim: To decrease the stage illumination.

Dionysian: The opposite principle to Apollonian, or, the creative, the imaginative, the spontaneous in art. Named for Dionysus, the Greek god of wine and fertility, whose festival, celebrated with drunkenness and licentiousness, is considered by many to be the birth of drama.

Dips: Electrical sockets set into the floor of the set, and usually covered by trap doors.

Directing: The art and technique of bringing the elements of theater together to make a play.

Director: The person who coordinates all aspects of the production, including the performances of the actors.

Director of Photography (DP): The person responsible for the camera crew and filming process, and makes decisions with the director. *(Also known as Cinematographer or First Cameraman)*

Director's Cut: Film that is slightly or drastically different from the final cut that the studio releases to the public.

Directors Guild of America (DGA): An entertainment organization that represents the interests of film and television directors in the United States. Founded as the Screen Directors Guild in 1936, the group merged with the Radio and Television Directors Guild in 1960 to become the Directors Guild of America. *(See Appendix: ENTERTAINMENT INDUSTRY ASSOCIATIONS/ORGANIZATIONS)*

Discover: To reveal a scene, a person, etc., to the audience, often by the opening of a curtain or bringing up stage lighting.

Discovery: A realization that takes place on stage due to information that was not available before.

Dissolve: A transition between shots which is done by layering them. The time the dissolve takes relates to a suggestion of the time passed between shots, such as rippled and blurred variants are used for flashbacks and memories.

DISSOLVE TO: Noted in a script, this is a common transition used when one scene fades out and the next scene fades into place, generally used to convey some passage of time.

Distance Shot: Used to show the actors or location from a distance, useful for establishing a scene. *(Also known as Extreme Long Shot or Extreme Wide Shot)*

Distanciation: In Brechtian performance, when actors maintain distance from their character by reminding the audience through often stylized gestures or behavior that they are simply people pretending, instead of trying to identify with their character.

Distortion: Noisy and unpleasant sound reproduction, usually the result of overloading sound equipment.

Distribution Arranger: Independent producers are not usually involved in the distribution of films and uses a company to provide that service.

Distribution Manager: The person responsible for supplying the physical elements for a production, including the legal elements such as copyright registration, rights documents insurance, copyright and title searches and talent agreements. *(Also known as Delivery Manager)*

Distributor: A company that exclusively handles the sales of a product to outlets for a certain territory.

Diva: Meaning goddess, it refers to an important female opera star, or a famous female singer of popular music. The masculine form is divo. Or, a self-important person who is temperamental and difficult to please.

DL: Abbreviation for Downstage Left. *(See Appendix: STAGE DIRECTION ABBREVIATIONS)*

DLC: Abbreviation for Downstage Left Center. *(See Appendix: STAGE DIRECTION ABBREVIATIONS)*

Documentary: A program that provides a factual record or report.

Dolby: Trade name for a series of noise reduction systems that have become standard on many film soundtracks.

Dolly: A piece of equipment used with the camera to allow for more mobility.

Dolly Grip: The person from the crew responsible for working with the dolly.

Dolly Shot: A moving camera shot that uses a wheeled camera platform known as a dolly.

Dolly Zoom: A camera special effect that undermines normal visual perception. A stationary object is filmed as the camera moves towards or away from it while adjusting its focal point so that the object remains the same size relative to the rest of the scene, accomplished by pulling the camera away from the focal object while zooming in at the same rate. *(Also known as Contra-Zoom or Hitchcock Zoom or Vertigo Effect)*

Dominate a Scene: To occupy an outstanding position on the stage, as the position farthest upstate, or on the highest plane of several levels. Or, a particularly strong actor who, intentionally or not, is the prime focus of a scene.

DOOD: *See Day-Out-of-Days.*

Doofer: An object or tool that you're not sure of the correct name for.

Door Flat: Frames into which a door is built.

Donut: A type of spot that has prerecorded material at the beginning and at the end with a hole in the middle for the voice part. The parts can be reversed as well, with the voice being the donut and the pre-recorded material in the hole.

Double: A person who is used in a place of a principal actor, usually for stunts or dangerous shots, but not to be confused with a stand-in.

Double Cast: Cast two actors in each part, either to provide an understudy, or to permit their appearance in alternate performances.

Double Entendre: A pun that can have two meanings, one usually provocative.

Double Exposure: Two distinct images appearing simultaneously with one superimposed upon the other. *(Also known as Superimposition)*

Double-Take: An exaggerated facial response to another actor's words or actions, where a performer looks, looks away, then quickly looks back again, usually used for comic effect.

Doubling: One actor taking more than one part in a production.

Down: The part of the stage toward the audience. *(Also known as Downstage)*

Down Camera Eye: The actor's eye that is closest to the camera.

Downgrade: Reduction of a performer's on-camera role from principal to extra.

Downlight: A light from directly above the acting area.

Downscale: Performers who appear in casual and regular clothing.

Downstage: The front half of the stage or the part closest to the audience. *(Also known as Down)*

Downstage Left (DSL): Towards the front of the stage on the left-hand side facing the audience.

Downstage Right (DSR): Towards the front of the stage on the right-hand side facing the audience.

Downtime: The time between shooting scenes.

DP: *See Director of Photography.*

DR: Abbreviation for Downstage Right. *(See Appendix: STAGE DIRECTION ABBREVIATIONS)*

Draft Script: A work in progress, which can go through any number of revisions before production.

Draftsman: Does sketches and drawings for costumes, sets and props.

Drama: The art of composing, writing, acting, or producing a literary composition intended to portray life or character or to tell a story usually involving conflicts and emotions exhibited through action and dialogue.

Dramatic: Relating to drama or the performance or study of drama.

Dramatic Force: Introduces the central conflict in the story. *(Also known as Exciting Force)*

Dramatic Irony: When the audience sees a character's mistakes or misunderstandings that the character himself is unable to see.

Dramatic Media: Telling of stories by way of stage, film, television, multimedia, radio, or computer.

Dramatic Play: Children's creation of scenes when they play pretend.

Dramatic Structure: The particular literary structure and style where plays are written.

Dramatic Unity: The principle of oneness, applicable to every aspect of dramatic writing and production, each element contributing to a single, overall effect.

Dramatis Personnae: From the Latin, meaning the characters in a play or the list of them.

Dramatist: The person who writes plays, also known as playwright.

Dramatists Guild of America (DG): The professional organization of playwrights, composers and lyricists, based in New York. *(See Appendix: ENTERTAINMENT INDUSTRY ASSOCIATIONS/ORGANIZATIONS)*

Dramatize: To convert a nontheatrical work into a play.

Dramaturg, Dramaturge: One who studies a play to interpret it for a company of actors or a director, answering questions about the text, the language, the period, the manners of the characters, the clothing, and the customs. They may share in selecting plays, revisions, adaptations, choosing translations, writing program notes, and advising technicians.

Dramaturgy: The art or technique of dramatic composition or representation.

Dramedy: A film, television, or multimedia show that combines both drama and comedy.

Drapery, Drapes: Any soft curtain material, hung, usually loosely, as part of the scenic decoration.

Draw Curtain: A curtain that divides in the middle so that it can be pulled to the sides of the stage.

Drawing Room Drama: Dramas, collectively or individually, that depict the social life of well-to-do people in a drawing room or similar setting.

DRC: Abbreviation for Downstage Right Center. *(See Appendix: STAGE DIRECTION ABBREVIATIONS)*

Dream Ending: What a character hopes will happen in the best of all worlds and as a direct result of his actions.

Dress: Dress rehearsal. Or, to costume a stage production. Or, to decorate a stage.

Dress Circle: In some theaters, a shallow gallery level above the main seating. *(Also known as Mezzanine or Royal Circle)*

Dressers: People responsible for helping performers to get in and out of their costumes during the show.

Dressing: Various items and props used on the set to make the scene look more realistic.

Dressing Room: Where an actor changes into costumes.

Dress Parade: Review by director/designer/wardrobe staff of all costumes worn by cast and paraded under stage lighting.

Dress Rehearsal: A principal rehearsal just before the show with the cast in full costumes.

Dress the Set: Adding items to add to the set, such as furniture and props.

Dress the Stage: Placing furnishings, pictures, and similar items to complete and balance a set.

Drift: A direction to an actor that they have moved out of position or off a mark.

Drive-on Pass: A pass to drive on and park at a studio.

Drive To: Money paid to an actor by a production company for driving to location other than a studio lot.

Driving: Taking over a scene and not letting other performers influence its direction.

Driving Double: Someone who is the same height, weight, hair color and age as the main actor. The viewer is lead to believe it is the main actor. *(Also known as Photo Double)*

Driving Question: The actor's objective in the active and very specific form of a question that needs to be answered in the scene. *(Also known as Actions or Essential Action or Intention or Motivating Drive or Objective)*

Drop: Fabric that is hung on the stage and often used in the actual show. Or, a quick fall to the floor.

Drop Box: A wooden box with a lid that opens downwards which can be opened remotely, which is used to drop lightweight objects onto the stage on a specific cue.

Dropped/Picked-up: When an actor is dropped from, then picked-up by payroll. This can only be done when there are ten working days between the drop and pick-up work dates and can only be done one time per actor per project.

Dropping Cues: Actors forgetting their lines or missing the cue.

Drop the Mic: Literally, the gesture of intentionally dropping a microphone at the end of a performance or speech to signal triumph. Figuratively, it is an expression of triumph for a successful event, and indicates a boastful attitude toward one's own performance. The gesture dates to the 1980s when it was used by rappers and comedians. *(Also known as Mic Drop)*

DRS: Abbreviation for Downstage Right. *(See Appendix: STAGE DIRECTION ABBREVIATIONS)*

Dry: An actor who forgets his words. Or, to record a sound without using any effect or other processing. Recording with an effect is recording wet.

Dry Ice: Frozen, solid carbon dioxide that produces a cloudy mist or fog when dropped into boiling water to create a fog effect on the set or stage.

Dry Run: A practice run, usually a technical run without actors.

Dry Tech: The rehearsal and setting of lighting, scenery, and sound cues, in preparation for the full technical rehearsal with actors.

Dry Up: Forget lines or business.

DS: Abbreviation for Downstage. *(See Appendix: STAGE DIRECTION ABBREVIATIONS)*

DSC: Abbreviation for Downstage Center. *(See Appendix: STAGE DIRECTION ABBREVIATIONS)*

DSL: Abbreviation for Downstage Left. *(See Appendix: STAGE DIRECTION ABBREVIATIONS)*

DSLC: Abbreviation for Downstage Left Center. *(See Appendix: STAGE DIRECTION ABBREVIATIONS)*

DSM: *See Deputy Stage Manager - Assistant Stage Manager.*

DSR: Abbreviation for Downstage Right. *(See Appendix: STAGE DIRECTION ABBREVIATIONS)*

Dual Dialog: When two characters speak simultaneously.

Dual Role: Two parts in a production that are played by the same actor.

Dub, Dubbing: Recording a voice in synch with a film image. Or, as an actor dubbing English onto a foreign film.

Dubbing Stage: The facility where the picture can be projected while the accompanying sound elements are mixed.

Ducat: Rhymes with bucket, a theater ticket. Or, a free admission pass.

Duet: An extended musical passage performed by two singers. They may or may not sing simultaneously or on the same musical line.

Dup, Dupe: An audio or video copy, short for duplicate.

Dutch Angle: A shot where the camera is set at an angle so the horizon line is not level, used to show a disoriented psychological state. *(Also known as Tilt Shot)*

E

Ear Prompter: Information transmitted to an earpiece through a loop around the neck. *(Also known as The Ear)*

Echo: A repeated sound received late enough to be heard as distinct from the source.

ECU: *See Extreme Close Up.*

Edit: In improv, the act of interrupting or ending a scene. Sometimes, the host or director will edit scenes to cut them short.

Editing: The process where strips of film are cut and joined together. *(Also known as Cutting)*

Editing Process: These steps make up the ordered editing process: Rushes/Dailies, Rough Cut, Fine Cut, and Final Cut.

Editor: The individual who assembles audio and visual components of the film. There may be several editors.

Editor's Cut: The first compilation of the show with the scenes in order. *(Also known as First Assembly or Rough Cut)*

Educational Theater: Theater conducted in or as an adjunct to schools. Also, theater with a didactic purpose.

Effects: *See Special Effects.*

Effects Spot: A spotlight that projects a slide, or a still, or moving picture, such as rain or clouds, onto the stage.

EGOT: An acronym for Emmy, Grammy, Oscar, and Tony, in reference to anyone who has won all four awards. From 1962 (the first) to 2014 (the most recent), there have only been 12 EGOT's, including actors Helen Hays, Rita Moreno, John Gielgud, Audrey Hepburn, Mel Brooks, Mike Nichols, and Whoopi Goldberg.

Electrician: The person usually responsible for all of the lighting on a stage or set.

Electronic Media: Means of communication characterized by the use of technology, such as radio, television, multimedia, and the internet.

Elevation: A working drawing usually drawn to scale, showing a view of a set or lighting rig. In general, the term refers to a front elevation. A rear elevation shows backs of scenic elements. A section elevation shows the side view.

Elevator Stage: A type of mechanized stage which has sections that can be raised or lowered.

Elizabethan Theater: The theater of England during the reign of Queen Elizabeth I. Also known as English Renaissance Theater or Early Modern English Theater, it refers to the theater of England between 1562 and 1642. This is the style of the plays of William Shakespeare, Christopher Marlowe and Ben Jonson.

Ellipsoidal: The most commonly used lighting instruments that feature a long light throw which creates a circular pool of light on the stage. *(Also known as ER Spotlights or Leko or Profile Spot)*

ELS: *See Extreme Long Shot.*

Embodying: Physically becoming something inhuman. For instance, one can embody a bird by flapping arms and squeaking or one can embody a table by going down to the floor on hands and knees.

Emcee (MC): The person who performs the role of host at an entertainment show or a large social occasion. *(Also known as Master/Mistress of Ceremonies)*

Emotion: The agitation of feelings such as sadness, power, fear, love, hate and joy. These feelings are usually followed by common responses such as: rapid heartbeat, crying or shaking.

Emotional Acting: Actors play their parts in such a way that they actually weep, suffer, or struggle emotionally as the character would. *(Also known as Subjective Acting)*

Emotional Memory: In method acting, when an actor attempts to draw upon memories of prior emotions to match the emotions of their character. *(Also known as Emotional Recall)*

Emotional Prep, Emotional Preparation: Ensures that an actor is prepared to be emotionally responsive to whatever they encounter during the production. By practicing coming from someplace specific and meaningful, to a different someplace specific and meaningful, the actor is trained to be prepared from the start.

Emotional Recall: The emotions from an actor's memory of personal experiences that are used to connect the actor to the character, and meet the emotional needs of the situation in the play or film. *(Also known as Emotional Memory)*

Emphasized Dialogue: Dialogue that the playwright or director wants stressed, usually identified with italics.

Employee For Hire: Contractual basis whereby a motion picture producer or company employs a composer or lyricist to create music or songs for a movie with copyright ownership to be retained by the producer or company.

Employer of Record: The company responsible for employment taxes and unemployment benefits.

Enact: To perform or act.

Encore: An additional performance, usually after a positive reception to the initial performance.

End Mark: Where an actor will end their move at the end of a scene. *(Also known as End Position)*

End On: Traditional audience seating layout where the audience is looking at the stage from the same direction.

Endowing: Assigning attributes to another performer's character.

Endowment: To give physical or emotional attributes to the character, to create more reality and meaning to further the needs of the story.

End Position: Where an actor will end their move at the end of a scene. *(Also known as End Mark)*

Engagement: An actor's period of employment in a part. Or, an arrangement for a company to play in a theater for a specified period of time.

Engineer: Individual who operates studio equipment during a recording.

Ensemble: A group of performers in the production.

Ensemble Acting, Ensemble Playing: Acting that stresses the total artistic unity of a group performance rather than individual performances.

Enter: To move onto the stage.

Entertainer: A person who entertains, such as an actor, a singer, comedian, dancer, or the like, especially a professional one.

Entr'acte: Meaning between acts, when orchestral music is played as the intermission ends and a musical or opera is about begin a new act. Or, brief entertainment provided during the intermission.

Entrance: A door or other access to the stage for actors. Or, the act of walking onto the stage in view of the audience.

Epic Theater: A form of theater based on the principle of using live performance as a means of social and political commentary. This started as a theatrical movement of the early 1920-30s characterized by the use of such artificial devices as cartoons, posters, and film sequences distancing the audience from theatrical illusion and following focus on the play's message. *(See Dialetical Theater or Theater of Alienation)*

Epilogue: A speech or short scene that sometimes follows the main action of a play.

Equity (AEA): Short for Actor's Equity Association, founded in 1913, the labor union representing actors and stage managers in the legitimate theater in the US. *(See Appendix: ENTERTAINMENT INDUSTRY ASSOCIATIONS/ORGANIZATIONS)*

ER Spotlight: The most commonly used lighting instruments that feature a long light throw which creates a circular pool of light on the stage. *(Also known as Ellipsoidal or Leko or Profile Spot)*

Escape Stairs: A means for an actor to get off a high level, etc., out of view of the audience.

Essential Action: A character's pursuit of a specific goal in a scene. Also referred to as the intention or driving question. *(Also known as Actions or Driving Question or Intention or Motivating Drive or Objective)*

Establish: When a person or object is established in the shot in a specific position or doing a specific action. Or, establishing a specific period of time.

Establishing Shot (EST): A view of a place which is used to tell the audience where they are.

Ethnically Ambiguous: A person's race is not easily defined by appearance.

Ethnic Types: Referring to the race of a person which is most often not Caucasian.

Evening Length Play: A play that constitutes a full evening of theater. *(Also known as Full-Length Play)*

eu: *See Close Up*.

Exclusive: The inability to do a commercial for a competing product once you have shot a commercial.

Executive Producer: The person responsible for the business side of the production, including funding. The individual who does the preparatory work for the film, such as securing rights and making deals with the studio.

Exeunt: An archaic stage direction calling for more than one person to exit, from the Latin — to go out.

Exeunt Omnes: A stage direction meaning the entire cast exits.

Exhibit E Sign In Sheet: SAG-AFTRA Audition Report which an actor fills out and initials upon arrival at a casting office.

Exit: A stage direction for an actor to leave the stage.

Exit Line: A line of dialogue spoken by an actor just before, or just as they leave the stage.

Exciting Force: Introduces the central conflict in the story. *(Also known as Dramatic Force)*

Explore and Heighten: In improv, to take an idea and see where it leads, exploring its natural consequences while simultaneously raising the stakes.

Exposition: Providing information about the plot, usually revealed in the first act, such as earlier events, the identity and relationship of the characters, or the present situation.

Expository Scene: A scene whose chief purpose is to provide exposition.

Expressionism: An extreme style of film which emphasizes the surreal in order to convey emotion, as well as subconscious thought.

EXT.: Short for Exterior, used in a screenplay to indicate a scene outside.

Extemporaneous: Impromptu, unrehearsed, unscripted.

Extending: Taking an idea and letting it become the central theme of the scene.

Extension: A technical note placed in the script, directly to the right of the character name that denotes how the character's voice is heard (e.g., O.S. is an extension that stands for Off-Screen).

Exterior, Exterior Shot: A scene filmed or taped outdoors.

External Technique: The outside-in approach to acting where an actor focuses first on what his or her character needs to do rather than what the character is thinking or feeling.

Extra: A non-speaking role in the production that is used in the background to create an atmosphere of the scene. *(Also known as Atmosphere or Background or Spear Carrier or Super or Supernumeraries or Xtra)*

Extravaganza: A spectacular presentation, with colorful costumes, and a large cast.

Extreme Close Up (ECU, XCU): A shot of a small piece of a subject, like the leg of a chair, or a subject's finger nail. *(Also known as Italian Shot)*

Extreme Long Shot (ELS): A shot which places action in context, and shows more than the actors. *(Also known as Distance Shot or Extreme Wide Shot)*

Extreme Wide Shot (EWS): A shot which places action in context, and shows more than the actors. *(Also known as Distance Shot or Extreme Long Shot)*

Eye Level Shot: Shot taken with the camera at human eye level, resulting in a natural effect on the audience.

Eye Line: The direction an actor should look off-screen to match a reverse angle or a point of view shot. It is best to give the actor an actual thing or spot to look at rather than a blank spot on an empty wall or an empty space in mid air.

Eye Line Match: A shot that cuts to an object then to a person.

F

Fabula Praetexta: An original play in Latin based on Roman legend or a historical event.

Fabulous Invalid: The theater, always amazingly vital despite its chronic financial and artistic setbacks.

Fade: The darkening of the screen until it is black creating a very strong transition, often between sequences. *(Also known as Fade Out or Fade to Black or Fade to Black Out)*

Fade In (F/I): The process where light is restored to a shot.

FADE IN: Used to start a script, in all CAPS.

Fade Out (F/O): The process where light is eliminated from a shot. *(Also known as Fade or Fade to Black or Fade to Black Out)*

FADE OUT: Used to end a script, in all CAPS.

Fade Out Lines: Lines that actors trail off rather than finishing.

Fade to Black: The darkening of the screen until it is black creating a very strong transition, often between sequences. *(Also known as Fade or Fade Out or Fade to Black Out)*

Fade to Black Out (FBO): The darkening of the screen until it is black creating a very strong transition, often between sequences. *(Also known as Fade or Fade Out or Fade to Black)*

Fake: Ad lib. Or, to omit lines or business.

Falling Action: The resulting action triggered by the climax, set in motion by a tragic force working against the hero.

False Proscenium: A frame formed by scenic canvas or vertical flat within the proscenium arch, used to reduce the size of the opening to put a small set onto a large stage.

False Stage: A special stage floor laid for a production, usually to support heavier than normal props.

False Start: A take where the talent makes an error within the first couple of lines. The take is usually stopped, and a new take is slated.

Fantasy: Ability to picture or create something without the benefit of experience.

Farce: A comedy with exaggerated characterizations, abundant physical or visual humor, and, an improbable plot.

Fast Fade To: The lighting and/or sound is faded out quickly.

Fast Stock: A type of film which is grainy and contrasty, and sometimes used for black and white filming.

Fat, Fat Part: A role, lines, or business offering an actor the opportunity to shine, or show what they can do.

Favor, Favor On: When the camera position throws more emphasis to one character over another.

Favored Nations: An agreement which means that all terms are equal among all primary actors.

Favor On: When the camera position throws more emphasis to one character over another.

FBO: *See Fade to Blackout.*

Feature Film: A film that is of full length, generally defined as any film at least one hour long and made primarily for distribution in theaters.

Featured: When an actor speaks five lines or less in a production.

Featured Role: A co-starring role where the actor may play a large role, but not the main character.

Featured Extra: When an extra is clearly visible on camera and not just a blur in the background.

Federal Communications Commission (FCC): An independent agency of the United States government that regulates interstate communications by radio, television, wire, satellite, and cable.

Fee: A royalty fee is charged per performance, with the amount depending on whether the producing company is professional or amateur.

Feed: Giving lines and action in such a way that another actor can make a point or get a laugh. *(Also known as Feeding)*

Feedback: A sharp whistle or rumble heard emanating from a sound system. It is caused by a sound being amplified many times. Or, a critique about a performance.

Feeding: Giving lines and action in such a way that another actor can make a point or get a laugh. *(Also known as Feed)*

f.g., Fg, FG: Abbreviation for Foreground.

FIA: *See International Federation of Actors.*

Fi-Core: Financial Core status is an option within the Screen Actors Guild (SAG-AFTRA) allowing actors to work both union and non-union jobs.

Field: The spread of light intensity across a beam.

Field Representative: A representative of the union that is responsible for making sure that standards are upheld.

Fight Choreographer: Creates and coordinates the combat and safety of the actors.

Fill Light: The light used to soften shadows.

Film: The process of making a movie by capturing a series of moving images. *(Also known as Filming or Filmmaking or Film Production)*

Film: A series of still images which, when shown on a screen, creates the illusion of moving images. *(Also known as Motion Picture or Movie or Photoplay or Theatrical Film)*

Film Editor: Edits the film and voice tracks.

Film Festival: A festival of short and/or feature-length films shown over the course of a few days to a few weeks.

the Film Foundation (TFF): An organization that educates the public about the importance of protecting and preserving film art, defends artists' work threatened with modification or distortion, and helps safeguard intellectual and cultural heritage. *(See Appendix: ENTERTAINMENT INDUSTRY ASSOCIATIONS/ORGANIZATIONS)*

Filming, Filmmaking: The process of making a movie by capturing a series of moving images. *(Also known as Film or Film Production)*

Film Noir: The dark detective genre of film which gained popularity in the 40s and 50s.

Film Production: The process of making a movie by capturing a series of moving images. *(Also known as Film or Filming or Filmmaking)*

Final Call: The final casting call for a production.

Final Cut: the final edited version of a film, approved by the director and producer.

Finale: The last song. Or, the closing ensemble of a musical production.

Final Mix: Recording a voice in sync with a film image.

Final Preview: Final performance before opening night.

Finding the Game: Whatever is interesting, unique, or strange about the scene. The relationship between the characters or the universe.

Finding Your Light: An actor's ability to sense when he or she is properly placed in respect to stage lighting.

Fire Curtain: Short for fireproof curtain.

Fine Cut: The version of the film where special effects and the mix are added.

Fire Exit: Particular exit from a building designated by local fire authority to be the correct means of escape from a part of the building in case of fire.

Fire in the Hole: An explosion or gunshot is ready to occur.

Fireproof Curtain: The foremost curtain in the proscenium arch, made of a nonflammable material on a steel frame, used to protect the auditorium if fire breaks out on or behind the stage.

Fireproofing: Treatment given to fabric, lumber, drapes, etc., to retard flammability.

First, First AD: *See First Assistant Director.*

First Assembly: The first compilation of the show with the scenes in order. *(Also known as Editor's Cut or Rough Cut)*

First Assistant Cameraman: Maintains and cleans all elements of the camera, attaches the camera to mounts, handles the lens, and pulls focus and/or zoom. *(Also known as Focus Puller)*

First Assistant Director: This is the director's right hand person, who stage manages the entire set and is responsible for giving most of the directions on the set to the cast and crew.

First Assistant Electrician: Supervises the lighting and electrical equipment.
(Also known as Best Boy or Best Girl)

First Cameraman: The individual who handles technical aspects of filming, such as lighting, lenses, etc., and works with the director on camera placement and movement. *(Also known as Cinematographer or Director of Photography)*

First Company Grip: Directs the crew of grips, many with specialized skills such as dolly grips, crane operators, or special equipment operators. *(Also known as Key Grip)*

First Culmination: The first decisive moment in which the character faces their highest obstacle so far.

First Mark(2nd, 3rd, etc.): Where an actor will start their move during a scene. *(Also known as First Position)*

First Night: The first date of a performance. *(Also known as Opening Night)*

First Position (2nd, 3rd, etc.): The place that is marked for the actor to start or stop on. *(Also known as First Mark)*

First Refusal: A request to hold an actor for a given day. It is not binding for either the producer or the actor. It is a sign of interest and not as good as a booking.

First Team: The actual principal cast members who are being used in a given scene.

First Unit: The part of the crew that works with the director to create the primary scenes.

Fish Eye Lens: An extreme wide-angle lens.

Fishpole: A microphone stand that cannot stand on its own, used to reach the actor out of view of the camera. *(Also known as a Boom Pole)*

Fit Up: The process of setting up the theater for the show.

the Five: Announcements are sometimes made to the audience into the auditorium and front of house informing them when the performance will begin. Calls may be made at the Half (30 min. before curtain up), the Quarter (15 min), the Five (5 min), and normally accompanied by bar bells, usually at 2 minutes before the performance begins.

Flag: To direct light and prevent unwanted reflection and lens flare on the camera.

Flap: In animation, movement of the character's mouth. If the talking stops and the character's mouth keeps moving, an actor will be called in to add verbiage so that the mouth flaps match the rhythm of the speech.

Flashback: The film technique where time continuity is broken, and events which happened prior are shown.

Flash Box: A small box containing the socket into which a pyro cartridge is plugged. *(Also known as Flash Pod)*

Flash Cut: An extremely brief shot, sometimes as short as one frame, which is nearly subliminal in effect. Also a series of short staccato shots that create a rhythmic effect.

Flashforward: Acting out a future or imagined event.

Flashing: What is said when taking a flash picture.

Flash Pan: A quick snap of the camera from one object to another that blurs the frame and is often used as a transition. Cuts are often hidden in swish pans, or they can be used to disorient or shock the audience.

Flash Pod: A small box containing the socket into which a pyro cartridge is plugged. *(Also known as Flash Box)*

Flats: A scenic element that is made up of a wood or metal frame and usually covered with stretched and painted cloth so that it appears to the audience to be a solid wall or surface.

Flexible Space: The areas used by audience and performer can be varied from one evening to the next or during the course of one evening.

Flies: The space above the stage where scenery and lighting can hang out of audience view. *(Also known as Fly Loft or Fly Tower)*

Float: A truck used for transporting scenery from theater to theater.

Floats: Footlights.

Flood: A type of light that gives widespread lighting. Or, to increase the beam size of a focus spot by moving the lamp and reflector towards the lens.

Floodlight: A lensless lighting instrument that produces a broad non-variable spread of light. Floodlights are used in battens, or singly to light large areas of the stage.

Floor Manager: In television or multimedia, the director's representative on the floor.

Floor Plan: All the elements of the scene setting and their arrangement.

Flown In: Scenery as it is lowered into view of the stage.

Flown Out: Scenery as it is raised out of view of the stage.

Fly: The action of lifting a piece of scenery or performers up (out) or down (in).

Fly Bars: The metal bars to which scenery and lamps are attached for flying above the stage.

Fly Floor: A narrow raised platform at the side of a stage in a theater where stagehands can control equipment in the flies.

Fly Gallery: High working platform at the side of the stage from which the flying lines are handled. Often are also the site for socket panels for connecting flown lighting apparatus to dimmers, and also sometimes a lighting position.

Fly Loft, Fly Tower: Extension of the stage walls up to allow scenery to be flown up until it is out of sight of the audience. The ideal fly tower should be more than twice the height of the proscenium arch. *(Also known as Flies)*

Fluffer: Person who readies adult movie actors on set in order to prepare them to perform.

FO, F/O: *See Follow on Cue.*

Focus: The discipline of an actor to concentrate and stay in character moment to moment so that nothing outside of the world of the play may influence their performance. Or, where a lighting instrument is pointed.

Focus Puller: Maintains and cleans all elements of the camera, attaches the camera to mounts, handles the lens and pulls focus and/or zoom. *(Also known as First Assistant Cameraman)*

Focus Through: A technique which changes the focus from one subject to another within the same shot. *(Also known as Rack Focus)*

Fog Machine: Electrically powered unit which produces clouds of white non-toxic fog, available in different smells, by the vaporization of mineral oil. *(Also known as Smoke Machine)*

FOH: *See Front of House.*

Foil, Foil Character: An acting role that is used for personality comparison, usually with the main character.

Foley: The sound effects that must synchronize with the picture.

Foley Artist: The member of the production crew who creates artificial sounds.

Foley Editor: The individual who combines and edits the sounds created by the Foley artist, so that they match the action captured on film.

Folio: A collection of songs offered for sale to the public.

Follow-on-Cue (FO, F/O): A cue timed to follow an original cue so quickly that it does not need a separate cue number.

Follow Shot: Shot in which the camera moves to follow the action.

Follow Spot: Powerful spotlight used to follow actors around the acting area.

Footlight: A lighting device arranged to illuminate a stage from the front edge of the stage floor in front of the curtain.

Forced Call: Making an actor or crew member come to work without the required turn-around time, which is less than 12 hours after they have finished.

Foreground: Whatever is between the camera and the subject of the picture.

Foreground Cross: When an extra crosses in front of the camera or principal actors.

Foreshadow: To hint, in dialogue or by other means, that some later dramatic action will occur.

Forestage: That part of the stage which projects from the proscenium into the auditorium. *(Also known as Apron)*

Form: The overall structure or shape of a work that frequently follows and established design.

Formal Theater: Focuses on public performance with an audience where the last performance is the most important.

Foreshadowing: A clue placed in the story early on that will help the reader understand why characters are acting the way they do or why certain elements are vital to the story.

Formal Production: The staging of a dramatic work for presentation for an audience.

Formula: More commonly used in film, it usually refers to a sure-fire method of structuring a script (i.e., the script must include certain elements and arrive at a certain ending).

Form Walk: A walk formed to deliver the essence of a character at the desired level of abstraction, based upon activity, and showing subjective and objective.

Foul: Ropes, cables, scenic pieces, etc., hanging from above, when they become tangled.

Found Space: A performance space that wasn't designed to be one, such as historic buildings, factories, public areas, etc.

Fourth Wall: The imaginary wall which separates the actors from the audience, and the audience from the stage. The actor uses it to create the reality in the scene.

Four-Walling: When the entertainer is responsible for most or all of the costs related to the show and the owner of the venue pays nothing, or almost nothing. In the most extreme cases, the entertainer also must rent the showroom. The owner then divides the profits with the entertainer in an agreed-upon split. *(Also known as Pay-to-Play)*

Frame: The base building block of film.

Framing: Crafting and sculpting individual moments for the purpose of highlighting them.

Freelance: Hired for just a week or short time of shooting.

French Scene: A section of a play between any entrance or exit of any character.

Freeze: To keep motionless, especially while the audience laughs, or to create a stage picture at the start/end of a scene.

Freeze Frame: A series of repeated frames creating the illusion of a still.

Freezing: In improv, to stop moving and speaking.

French Scene: A scene division within a play marked by the entrance or exit of an actor.

Frequency: The number of times a sound source vibrates each second. Or, how often a production schedules performances or showings.

Fresnel Light: A lens that produces a wider, soft-edged beam of light, which is commonly used for back light and top light.

Freytag's Triangle: Rising action, crisis or climax, perhaps a realization (epiphany), then a falling off or dénouement, and closure which is the classic structure of traditional narrative.

From the Top: To start the scene over from the beginning. *(Also known as Back-to-One or Reset, or To Ones)*

Front Light: A lighting unit placed somewhere in the auditorium for the illumination of the front of the stage.

Front of House (FOH): Area of theater and people who deal with the audience, such as the ushers, box office, etc.

Front of House Calls: Announcements are sometimes made to the audience into the auditorium and front of house informing them when the performance will begin. Calls may be made at the Half (30 min. before curtain up), the Quarter (15 min), the Five (5 min), and normally accompanied by bar bells, usually at 2 minutes before the performance begins.

Frost: A diffusing filter that softens the edges of a light beam.

Full Drop: Any drop curtain other than a cut drop.

Full Front: Actor position facing the audience.

Full House: The entire audience section is filled to capacity.

Full-Length Play: A play that constitutes a full evening of theater. *(Also known as Evening Length Play)*

Full Production: A performance that includes all the elements of live theater: lights, costumes, props, makeup, design and audience. In opera, this includes music provided by an orchestra or piano along with the characters' singing.

Full Shot (FS): Fills the frame with the actor from head to toe, with the emphasis more on action and movement rather than a character's emotional state.

Full Stage: A stage used in its entirety for setting and acting.

Future Release: A play or dramatic property that is not yet available for license.

FX: *See Special Effects.*

G

GA: *See General Admission.*

Gaffer: The person in charge of electric components on set during set-up, takedown, etc. *(Also known as Chief Electrician or Head Electrician or Key Electrician)*

Gaffer Tape: Used for marking out areas or temporarily securing almost anything on the set.

Gagging: Trying to make a joke or do something funny that doesn't flow naturally from the scene.

Gallery: The highest section of the theater, without seats, where people can stand to watch a performance.

Gang: A grouping of lighting or sound equipment.

General Admission (GA): A charge made for admission to a movie or performance. Or, unreserved seating.

General American Accent: When filming takes place in the US, but casting may be further reaching, and the background breakdown states it needs a general American feel.

General Interview: Interviewed by a casting director, producer, etc., with the intention of simply getting to know you, for future consideration.

General Release: A document the talent signs that gives the filmmaker permission to distribute and sell the film. *(Also known as Talent Release)*

Generation: The process whereby each time you copy a piece of film or tape, it losses some clarity.

Genre: The category a story or script falls into (i.e., the main types of storyline, principally tragedy and comedy), along with the multitude of sub-categories. *(See Appendix: PERFORMING ARTS GENRES)*

George Spelvin: A fictitious name, dating from the late 1800s, traditionally used in theater programs to conceal the identity of an actor doubling in a second role.

Gesture: A specific physical action that communicates emotion, information, or attitude.

Get In: Setting up the theater for the show.

Get-Offs: A means for an actor to get off a rostrum, high level, etc., out of view of the audience.

Ghost: A singing voice used for another actor.

Ghost Light: A light left on the stage overnight and/or when the stage is not in use for safety. It also has superstitious meaning. *(See Appendix: THEATER SUPERSTITIONS)*

Give a Level: A request from the sound mixer that the actors speak a sample to set the sound level on their equipment.

Given Circumstances: The background and current circumstances of a character, ranging from who they are, where they are, and why they are doing it. The costumes, sets and lighting—all the circumstances that are given to the actor. Or, the who, what, when, where, and why of a play/film.

Giving the Scene: Shifting audience attention from one actor to another.

Glaze: Glossy transparent or semitransparent finish applied as a final coat to a painted stage floor or to scenery to soften its appearance.

Glib Thru: A rehearsal with actors going through the lines of the play as quickly as possible, picking up the cues.

Glow Tape: Luminous yellow self-adhesive tape used to mark floors so that positions can be found in blackouts.

Go: The action word used by stage managers to cue other technical departments.

Goal: What the character wants to achieve.

Gobo: Thin metal plate cut out in a pattern and placed in a lantern to project pattern or shape into the acting area.

God Mic: Slang for a PA system setup for a director to use in a large venue to talk to everyone on stage without shouting, during rehearsals and technical periods. Also used in some small or experimental spaces for tech crew to talk to actors or other crew, if no headset system is available.

Gofer: A junior member of the crew who is given instructions to fetch and carry equipment, tools, do errands, etc. *(Also known as Production Assistant or Runner)*

Going Dark: Warning to people on stage that the lights are about to be switched off. Normally said during lighting plotting sessions or technical rehearsals.

Going Up: When the actor forgets their line during a rehearsal, they will indicate they are Up. *(Also known as Up)*

Golden Hour: The period shortly before sunset during which daylight is redder and softer.

Golden Time: The 16th hour on the shooting day. Extras receive base pay for every single hour spent on set past this point, equal to one's 8-hour daily rate every hour.

Gold Record: A single or album that has sold 500,000 units, certified by the Recording Industry Association of America.

Goosebumps Walkaway: The moment when a man says a line to a woman (or one character to another) so deep, moving, or powerful, that gives her goosebumps, before he walks away forever. A well-known classic example is in the 1940s movie Casablanca, when Humphrey Bogart said to Ingrid Bergman, "Here's looking at you kid."

Go See: A performer visiting a client to investigate what a particular job entails.

Gossip: Talking about things that are offstage.

GOTE : An acronym (Goal, Obstacle, Tactics and Expectation) used to remind actors of their character development.

Go Up: When a show starts and the curtain goes up.

Grand Circle: The balcony with tiered seating above the stalls. *(Also known as Circle)*

Grand Dame: An actress who plays the role of an imperious elderly woman. Or, an actress who specializes in such roles.

Grand Finale: A finale on a grand spectacular scale, where the principals and ensemble participate, usually referring to musical productions.

Grand Guignol: Pronounced grahn ghee-nyoll, a French term, derived from the name of a Paris theater where short, sensational horror plays were performed.

Graveyard Slots: Programs that are broadcast on television at times when the fewest viewers are tuned in, such as 2-6 a.m., especially on a Sunday morning.

Greasepaint: Make up usually supplied in stick form, for application to the face or body.

Great White Way: A nickname for a section of Broadway in midtown Manhattan, specifically the portion that encompasses the theater district, named such because of all the dazzling theater lights.

Greek Theater: Theatrical events in honor of the god Dionysus in ancient Greece and included play competitions and a chorus of masked actors.

Green Light, Green Lit: When a project has been approved for production, usually meaning it has been funded.

Green Room: A room where performers relax before going on stage.

Green Screen: A blank screen which acts as the backdrop to live action. Special effects and visuals are added.

Grid: The support structure close to the top of the fly tower where the pulleys of the flying system are supported. Or, arrangement of scaffolding where lamps are hung in a performance space with no flying facilities.

Gridded: Any flying piece raised into the flies.

Grip: Crew member who handles, carries, moves, and stores lighting, electrical, and other equipment on the set. *(Also known as Hammer Grip)*

Groucho: When an actor needs to crouch a bit as he approaches the camera because the cameraman can't tilt up and still focus.

Groundling: Poorer members of the audience in an Elizabethan theater who occupied the sections of the theater at ground level, just in front of the performance space.

Ground Plan: Scaled plan showing the exact position, seen from above, of all items standing on the stage floor or set and indicating the position of items suspended above.

Ground Row: A long piece of scenery at the base of a backcloth usually to mask the very bottom of a cloth or lamps lighting a cloth. Or, compartmentalized floodlight battens at floor level used to light the bottom of sky drapes, etc.

Group Shot (GR/SH): A shot that shows a large group of people. *(Also known as Crowd Shot)*

Group Theater: Founded by Harold Clurman, Cheryl Crawford and Lee Strasberg in the 1930s, the Group Theater based its acting on the innovative teachings of Konstantin Stanislavski. A renowned American theatrical company whose members included Lee Strasberg, Stella Adler, and Sandford Meisner, it was based on an ensemble approach to acting and changed the course of American theater.

Groove: Rhythm or tempo that helps create the feel of the performance.

Gun Mic: A highly directional condenser microphone.

Guest Star: Usually when a celebrity or well-known actor plays a secondary role in a television or multimedia series.

Gypsy: A dancer/singer in musical theater, typically in the chorus, who moves from show to show to show.

H

Hair and Makeup: The department that handles the hair and makeup for the performers, and makes sure they stay consistent throughout the production.

the Half: Announcements are sometimes made to the audience into the auditorium and front of house informing them when the performance will begin. Calls may be made at the Half (30 min. before curtain up), the Quarter (15 min), the Five (5 min), and normally accompanied by bar bells, usually at 2 minutes before the performance begins.

Half Hour: The time before a performance when all actors must be present in the theater, traditionally a half an hour before curtain up.

Ham: An actor who gives a very artificial, broad or exaggerated performance.

Hammer Grip: Moves everything on the set except lighting equipment and cables. *(Also known as Grip)*

Hand: Applause.

Hand-Held Camera, Hand-Held Shot: This moving camera technique is often used to bring the viewer into the action through subjective shots.

Handle: The premise for a scene.

Hand Props: Objects used to help tell a story that are often small and hand carried during performances (e.g., glasses, wallet, scarf, etc.).

Hang: To suspend any piece of scenery or equipment, such as lights.

Hanging Plot: A listing of all the flying scenery and what is on each piece, prepared by the technical director or the stage manager.

Happiness: The character's long term objective or big dream in life. It also helps in providing conflict and dimension to every scene. *(Also known as Super Objective)*

Hard Blacks: Black-covered scenic flats used as masking.

Harmony: The combination of musical notes to form chords that serve to enhance the melody line as in the art of combining notes into chords.

Head and Shoulder Shot (H&S): The standard shot when there are two subjects engaged in conversation, which frames a person from the chest up.

Head Arrangements: An arrangement devised spontaneously where no chords are prepared for instrumentalists and vocalists. Instead, they read off lead sheets and an arrangement is made from various experimental styling devised at the studio.

Headbook: The sheet, poster or book of headshots an agent sends to a prospective client interested in using one of their clients. *(Also known as Headsheet)*

Head Electrician: The person in charge of electric components on set. *(Also known as Chief Electrician or Gaffer or Key Electrician)*

Header: An element of a shooting script, occupying the same line as the page number on every page, and includes the date of the revision and the color of the page.

Head Fly: The head of the fly crew who are responsible for lifting scenery or other objects above the stage.

Headliner: A performer whose name appears most prominently in a program or advertisement or on a marquee and is the star of the show.

Heads: A shouted warning for staff to be aware of activity above them or when an object is being dropped from above. *(Also known as Heads Up)*

Headsheet: The sheet, poster or book of headshots an agent sends to a prospective client interested in using one of their clients. *(Also known as Headbook)*

Headshot: A photograph a performer uses to showcase their look.

Heads Out: The way a reel-to-reel tape is stored, with the loose end at the beginning of the tape, enabling the tape to be played immediately.

Heads Up: A shouted warning for staff to be aware of activity above them or when an object is being dropped from above. *(Also known as Heads)*

Heart-Throb: A young, attractive male performer with a large fan base.

Hemp: A type of rope used for flying, made from fibers found within the bark of the cannabis plant.

Hemp Set: The simplest flying system consisting of a series of hemp ropes threaded through pulleys on the grid, and tied off on the fly floor on a cleat. The usual arrangement is for three ropes to be attached to a flying piece, named by their position relative to the fly floor — short, center and long.

Hero Prop: A prop with special importance, often needing special handling by the actor.

Hiatus: Time when the cast and crew of a television or multimedia series is in between production.

High: So emotionally intense or passive, the actor cannot respond.

High Angle Shot: From above eye level, this shot can have the effect of making the character seem weak or frightened.

High-Key: When light brilliantly illuminates a set.

High Note: The highest note sung in a particular song which varies according to the musical key of the song.

High-Speed Dub: A copy that is made at several times normal speed, often used in reference to tape duplication, often less costly with a quicker turn-around time than real time or at speed dubs, but can be susceptible to problems.

High Spot: A camera angle that looks down on the subject.

History Play: A play dealing with a historical subject, such as Shakespeare's Henry IV and Richard II.

Histrionics: Any dramatic representation, although more frequently to mean over-emotional acting.

Hit: To emphasize a word or line with extra force. Or, a great popular success.

Hitchcock Zoom: An unsettling camera special effect that appears to undermine normal visual perception. A stationary object is filmed as the camera moves towards or away from it while adjusting its focal point so that the object remains the same size relative to the rest of the scene, accomplished by pulling the camera away from the focal object while zooming in at the same rate. Nicknamed the Hitchcock Zoom for famed writer/director/producer Alfred Hitchcock (1899-1980) who first used the special effect, conceived by Irmin Roberts, a second-unit cameraman, in his movie Vertigo. *(Also known as Contra-Zoom or Dolly Zoom or Vertigo Effect)*

Hit Your Mark: A direction to the actor to stand in the exact spot designated.

HL: Abbreviation for House Left. *(See Appendix: STAGE DIRECTION ABBREVIATIONS)*

Hoedown: In improv, refers to a song structure made popular by the television show Who's Line Is It Anyway. It's a simple melody, with 4 lines to a verse, and no chorus. Rhyme pattern in the verse is usually ABCB.

Hold: When an actor is being paid, but is not working. Or, to pause while acting for audience reaction.

Holding, Holding Area: The area or bus set aside for extras to wait between scenes on a set or location.

Holding Fee: Set payment by an advertiser to retain the right to use a performer's services, images or likeness on an exclusive basis.

Holding for Laughs: Waiting for the audience to quiet down after a funny line or scene.

Holding the Book: When a member of the crew assists performers by giving them their lines.

Hold Over: When a director decides to use an actor for an extra day not originally scheduled.

Hollywood: An ethnically diverse, densely populated neighborhood, notable as the home of the US film industry, including several of its historic studios, and its name has come to be a shorthand reference for the industry and the people in it.

Honeywagon: A number of dressing rooms and mini-bathrooms attached together and pulled by a tractor trailer to a shooting location.

Hoofer: A dancer, especially a tap dancer.

Hook: A phrase or melody line that repeats itself in a song and is usually the catchy part of a song. Or, the part of the plot in a movie or show that sets it apart from the competition. Or, a hook on a pole used to pull an unwanted performer off the stage on amateur night in a variety show.

Host: The person who welcomes the audience and introduces the actors.

Hot Camera: A camera that is on.

Hot Mic: A microphone that is turned on.

Hot Points: The crew yells this as they move equipment.

Hot-Seating: A way of deepening character development by answering questions from anyone or a group while in role.

Hot Set: A set where furniture, props, and sometimes food are positioned for an imminent shoot, so called to prevent those items from being moved and thus compromising continuity in the finished product.

Hot Spot: A stage area that is brightly lit. Or, reflections on shiny surfaces, which must be eliminated because they will generally produce a region of white in the final film.

House: Audience in the theater. Or, the venue itself.

House Left: When facing the stage, the left side of the theater.

House Lights: Lights that are used to light the auditorium.

House Manager: The person responsible for anything to do with the audience.

House Open: When the audience is being seated before the show and performers can no longer appear on the stage.

House Right: When facing the stage, the right side of the theater.

House Tape: A voice demo that includes short samples of all talent represented by a certain agent.

HR: Abbreviation for House Right. *(See Appendix: STAGE DIRECTION ABBREVIATIONS)*

Hypokrites: The Greek word meaning actor.

I

Idiot Cards: The large flash cards that have a performer's script printed on them. *(Also known as Cue Cards)*
Idol: A performer regarded with adoration or devotion.
If-Come Deal: The major players are already pre-signed for a pilot and will start if/when the network gives the go ahead.
Image: The casting type or quality the performer portrays to the theatrical community or to the public.
Image Size: The literal size of the image, as seen by the viewer, such as the farther the subject, the smaller it is, and vice-versa.
Imaginary Line: The rule that action must move across the screen in the same direction across shots placed in sequence in order to preserve continuity. *(Also known as the 180° rule)*
Imagination: Ability to picture or create from one's own experience or thought.
Immediacy: The need to accomplish an objective within a short period of time.
Immediate Objective: What the character is trying to achieve within a scene or monologue.
Impersonator: An actor who impersonates specific people as a form of entertainment.
Impresario: An entrepreneur who sponsors entertainment. Or, the general director of an opera company.
Improv: Improvisation, especially as a theatrical comedy technique.
Improv Audition: An audition where the actor is not given a script, but is given a topic and they must make up their own script based on that topic.
Improvisation: Coming up with actions and/or lines on the spot without any preparation.
Impulse: A natural response that an actor responds to in the moment.
Inciting Incident: An event that is the catalyst for the action of a play.
In-Development: When a book or spec screenplay has been optioned or bought and pre-production starts.
Indicate: To project that which character does not feel.

Indicating: Unrealistic acting, such as showing what your character is feeling or doing without really feeling or doing, leading to a false and shallow performance.

Indirect Presentation: When the audience sees a character's mistakes or misunderstandings that the character himself is unable to see.

Industrial: Film, short or a video clip used for educational and training purposes only.

Inflection: The variation in the pitch of an actor's voice as he reveals emotion.

Informal Production: The exploration of all aspects of a dramatic work in a setting where experimentation is emphasized.

Informal Theater: A theatrical performance that focuses on small presentations, such as one taking place in a classroom setting, usually not intended for public view.

In Four: A scene played in an acting area bounded on the upstage side by an imaginary line across the stage from the left wing farthest upstage to the right wing furthest upstage, and on the downstage in the In Three area.

Ingenue: A female lead between the ages of 16-30.

Initial Incident: The first most important event in a play from which the rest of the play develops.

Ink: To sign a contract.

Inner Action: A physical action by the actor in the pursuit of an objective (e.g., to attack, to soothe, etc.).

Inner Life, Inner Monologue: A character's active, imaginative inner thoughts while the actor is playing a role.

In One: Usually a stage blocking term, it's the acting area just upstage of the curtain line, and downstage of the first vertical side leg. Many entrances in the theater occur down right, or in one. Also said of a curtain position at the same line, so to play a scene "in one" usually means to play it on the downstage area in front of the curtain, usually while scenery is being changed behind the curtain.

Insert: A form of pick-up where a short segment of the script is reread from one point to another.

Inserts: A shot that is used in the footage during post-production that includes tiny sections of close-up action used to illustrate specific points, such as a finger dialing a telephone, which would get lost in a wider view.

Inset: A small scene set inside a larger one.

Instant Trouble: In improv, starting the scene with an offer that creates a problem or a conflict.

Instigating Action: A specific thing has been said or done to cause the performer to respond at that very instant a monologue begins.

Instinct: A compelling or powerful impulse.

Institute: To project an impulse that elicits a response.

Instrument: The actor's collective working of the body, voice, mind, and imagination.

Instrument: A light. *(Also known as Lantern or Luminaire)*

Insurance: The additional take filmed, even though there is one that seems good enough, just in case. *(Also known as One for Safety or Protection or Safety)*

INT.: Short for Interior, a term used in a screenplay to indicate a scene taking place inside.

Intelligent Light: An automated lighting instrument where certain functions such as panning, tilting, focusing, dimming, beam shaping and coloring, etc., are motorized and remotely operated from a control console.

In-Tension: Moving with the body tensed.

Intention: An acting objective, or action, that an actor pursues while onstage. *(Also known as Actions)*

Interactive Theater: Any form of theater in which the audience is not a passive performer. Encompasses a range of different styles, ranging from improv to loosely-scripted stories such as murder mysteries or faux events.

Interior Shot: A scenic shot inside a sound stage or inside a set on location.

Intermission: A break between acts in a stage performance. *(Also known as Interval)*

International Federation of Actors (FIA): A global federation of performers' trade unions, guilds and professional associations. Founded in 1952, it represents hundreds of thousands of performers with 90 member organizations in 60+ countries around the world. *(See Appendix: ENTERTAINMENT INDUSTRY ASSOCIATIONS/ORGANIZATIONS)*

Interpolation: Dialogue, song, or stage business inserted into a script by a performer or director, which is illegal in copyrighted works without the permission of the author or their representative.

Interval: A break between acts in a stage performance. *(Also known as Intermission)*

In the Can: A film or scene that has been filmed to the satisfaction of the director and is therefore considered complete.

In-The-Round: A theater where the audience is seated on all four sides of a central stage.

In the Wings: Off left or off right between the side curtains and just out of view of the audience. Usually an actor who is in the wings is waiting for their entrance, or has just made their exit from the stage. Or, anyone who is ready to do something or to be used at the appropriate time.

In Three: A scene played in an acting area bounded on the upstage side by an imaginary line drawn across the stage from the left wing to the right wing three-quarters of the way upstage.

In-Time: The start time for a day of shooting.

Intonation: The rising and falling of voice in speech.

Introductory Shot: When a sequence of the subject is shot doing other things and added to the final film, it makes the person seem more interesting.

Iris: A technique used to show an image in only one small round area of the screen. An iris can be either a transitional device using the image held as a point of transition, or a way of focusing attention on a specific part of a scene without reducing the scene in size.

Iris-In: Moves inward from all sides to leave only a small image on the screen.

Iris-Out: Begins as a pinpoint and then moves outward to reveal the full scene.

Iron: A curtain of fireproofed material that covers the entire proscenium opening and acts as a firebreak between the stage and the auditorium. *(Also known as Safety Curtain)*

Isolation: Moving one part of the body only.

Issue: To leave the stage.

Italian Shot: Emphasizes a small area or detail of the actor, such as the hands or mouth, or of the eyes. *(Also known as Extreme Close Up Shot)*

J

Jack-Knife Set: A stage or set used for rapid scene-shifting, consisting of a platform or two on casters, pivoted at one corner to swing off and on set.

J-Card: The artwork on a dvd, etc., type box, named for the shape it makes when folded to fit in the box.

Jeer: To make rude and mocking remarks, typically in a loud voice.

Jingle. A short phrase of music, usually accompanied by lyrics used to convey a commercial message.

the Jonesy: The first shot of the day which honors assistant cameraperson Sarah Jones, who lost her life on the set of the film Midnight Rider.

Journeyman Actor: An experienced and competent, routine performer. (i.e., commercial actors, voiceover performers, stunt doubles, stand-ins, extras, etc.

Jukebox Musical: A stage musical that has been constructed from pre-released songs, usually from one artist or genre.

Jump: To accidentally skip lines of dialogue. Or, a raised work platform within the stage house.

Jump Cut: An instantaneous cut from one action to another, at first seemingly unrelated action because of the abrupt change in time and/or place.

Jumper Cable: An extension cable with a stagepin head.

Jump the Shark, Jumping the Shark: An idiom to describe the moment a series begins a decline in quality, signaled by a particular scene, or episode, where the writers use some type of gimmick in an attempt to keep viewers' interest. This originated from a 1970s Happy Days sitcom episode where the character Fonz, played by Henry Winkler, jumped a shark on waterskis.

Junket: Press releases, advertising campaigns, merchandising, franchising, media and interviews with the key people involved with the making of the film.

Justifying: In improv, finding a solution for every offer and every element introduced in the scene.

Juve, Juvenile: A male lead between the ages of 16-30.

K

Kabuki: One of the traditional forms of Japanese theater, originating in the 1600s and combining stylized acting, costumes, makeup, and musical accompaniment.

Katharsis: The feeling of release at the end of a tragedy experienced by audience members who have undergone feelings of fear and pity, shared in the troubles of the play's protagonist, and now are set free from the emotional grip of the action. Aristotle called this cleansing the pleasure of tragedy. *(Also known as Catharsis)*

Kennedy Center Honors: An annual honor given to those in the performing arts for their lifetime of contributions to American culture (although recipients do not need to be US citizens). The honors have been presented annually since 1978 in the Kennedy Center Opera House in Washington DC.

Key: A fixed point used by the actor to remember a position without marks. Or, a direction to use a particular element of a scene to reinforce an actor's performance. Or, the spiritual value of a play or film.

Key _______: This word designates someone as a supervisor/manager.

Key Electrician: The person in charge of electric components on set. *(Also known as Chief Electrician or Gaffer or Head Electrician)*

Key Grip: Directs the crew of grips, many with specialized skills such as dolly grips, crane operators, or special equipment operators. *(Also known as First Company Grip)*

Key Light: The primary light specifically illuminating the subject.

Key Makeup Artist: Designs and applies makeup to actors, organizes and supervises operation of all personnel in the makeup department, including hairdressers, body makeup artists and makeup assistants.

Key Second Assistant Director: Responsible for having extras on set at the right time, blocking extras into crowd scenes, cueing of extras, etc. *(Also known as Senior Second Assistant Director)*

Kicker Light: This type of light is placed opposite the key light in order to rim and separate the subject from the background.

Kill: To switch off a light or sound effect. Or, to remove a prop. Or, success for a comedian or comedy.

Kill the Baby: When the Fresnel light is turned off.

Klak: A group of people hired to lead the applause. *(Also known as Claque)*

Klieglight: Not used much today, but often referring to any powerful spotlight unit. Originally, a carbon arc spotlight developed by John and Anton Klieg, and used extensively in Hollywood.

L

L: Abbreviation for Left Stage. *(See Appendix: STAGE DIRECTION ABBREVIATIONS)*

Label: A record company.

Ladder: Non-climbable structure in the shape of a ladder where instruments can be hung in a vertical stack.

Lantern: A light. *(Also known as an Instrument or Luminaire)*

Larynx: The human voice box containing the vocal chords.

Lash: To pull two flats together, edge to edge, by winding a lash line over lash line cleats in back.

Lash Line: A rope line used to fasten flats or other scenic units to one another.

Last Looks: The moment just before shooting starts when the hair-makeup-prop people make sure that the actors and the set look exactly as they should.

Laugh Curve: The audience's reaction that actors listen for in order to anticipate the length of time the audience will laugh.

Laugh Line: A line of dialogue calculated to produce a laugh from the audience.

Laugh Track: The laughter of a live audience of a situation comedy or other television or multimedia show that actors are performing in front of that is recorded and played back when the show is aired.

Laundry List: A long series of copy points in a script.

Lavalier Microphone: Originally, a mic worn around the neck on a string. Now applies to a small tie-clip microphone.

Lay an Egg: A production or performance that fails miserably.

Lay 'Em in the Aisles: To make an audience laugh hysterically.

LC: Abbreviation for Left Center Stage. *(See Appendix: STAGE DIRECTION ABBREVIATIONS)*

LCS: Abbreviation for Left Center Stage. *(See Appendix: STAGE DIRECTION ABBREVIATIONS)*

Lead: Role with the most significant part.

Leader: Conductor or person in charge of the band.

Leading Lady: The actress playing the largest role in the cast.

Leading Man: The actor playing the largest role in the cast.

Lead Role: A starring role in a production.

Lead Sheet: A musical notation of a song's melody along with the chord symbols, words and other pertinent information.

Leader Tape: Reel-to-reel tape which contains songs separated by white tape for easy access.

Leading Center: The body part or feature used by an actor to lead movements, often used to reflect a character's major personality trait.

League Of Resident Theatres (LORT): The largest professional theater association of its kind in the United States and issues contracts with Actor's Equity regarding the payment and treatment of actors.

Leak: When the crack between two flats lashed together lets light through, or when a lighting instrument's beam is not properly channeled by barn doors or a top hat.

Left: Refers to the stage from an actor's point of view, not from that of the audience.

Left Frame: Indicates the side of the shot where the performers are kept from the camera operator's perspective. *(Also known as Camera Left)*

Legit, Legit Acting: Refers to acting for theater, film, television, and multimedia, but not commercials or industrial.

Legitimate Theater: Professionally produced stage plays as distinguished from films, variety shows, or theme park performance.

Legs: Masking curtains hung vertically on the sides of the performing area and hide offstage areas from the view of the audience. *(Also known as Tormentors or Torms)*

Leko: The most commonly used lighting instruments that feature a long light throw which creates a circular pool of light on the stage. *(Also known as Ellipsoidal or ER Spotlights or Profile Spot)*

Level: The height of an actor's head as determined by his or her body position. Or, a request from the sound mixer that the actors speak a sample so they can set the sound level on their equipment.

Librarian: In charge of preparing the music for the orchestra. Scores are usually rented and have to be annotated to reflect cuts and other changes for a given production.

Library Shot: A shot made of pre-existing footage. *(Also known as Stock Shot)*

Libretto: A book or script of a musical or opera production.

License: A legal permit. Or, to authorize by legal permit.

Lick: A brief, improvised musical interpolation.

Lift: The orchestra pit and/or sections of the stage may be mounted on lifts to make moving of heavy items (e.g., piano, etc.) easier. Sometimes the forestage doubles as the orchestra pit by use of a lift.

Light Board: Computer or hand-operated board that houses the controls for the stage lights.

Light Cues: A change in the stage lighting.

Light Curtain: A lighting effect which, when an area is diffused with smoke, produces a wall of light. Automated versions are available which have color changers built-in and are able to tilt up and down.

Lighting Department: This includes the lighting designer, head electrician, lighting operator, etc.

Lighting Designer: The person responsible for a show's lighting.

Lights-Camera-Action: The traditional legendary cue to the members of a film crew at the beginning of a take, though the actual pre-take cues are more detailed than this, such as:

1st Assistant Director (AD): Roll sound!

Boom Operator/Sound Mixer: Sound speed!

1st AD: Roll camera!

1st Assistant Camera (AC): Camera speed, hit it.

2nd AC: [Calls out scene designation]. Marker!

Slate gets clapped, 2nd AC moves away —

Camera Operator: Set.

Director: Action!

Lime: Now known as Follow Spot, Lime is an antiquated term, from the days of stage lighting before electricity, produced by directing a flame at a piece of calcium oxide, or quicklime.

Limelight: One who is the center of attention, derived from when stage lighting was often produced by directing a flame at a piece of calcium oxide, or quicklime, before electricity.

Limited Engagement: A run of performances in a particular venue with a definite end date.

Line: Each time a character speaks.

Line Cue: The last portion of the last line before the cue begins.

Line Producer: The person responsible for keeping the director on budget and on schedule, concerned with the day-to-day details of finishing a project or just keeping the project moving forward smoothly and on schedule.

Line Rehearsal: A rehearsal for spoken lines rather than for body movements.

Lines: Scripted dialogue.

Line Up: When the director, director of photography, and actors go through a scene to establish camera positions.

Lip Flap: When a movie's sound and picture are out of synchronization.

Little Theater: Any small theater, but especially one for amateur productions, often with experimentation.

Live Industrial: Live performances for corporations, sometimes about their products or services.

Loader: The person who takes care of film stock and uses the clapboard. *(Also known as Second Assistant Cameraman)*

Load-In, Load Out: The process of bringing the set into or out of the theater. Or, building set pieces.

Local: A commercial airing in only one city, generally close to where it is cast.

Local Casting Director: Handles casting in the area where a film is about to shoot.

Local Hire: An actor or crew member hired locally when on location.

Local Light: A light source found in the scene.

Local Music: Music coming from another source in the scene.

Location: The stage, set or area where filming is taking place.

Location Sound Engineer: Responsible for all sound recording on the set during the production. *(Also known as Production Sound Mixer or Sound Mixer)*

Locked Cut, Locking the Cut: The point after which no further changes in the visual aspects of the show are made.

Lock it Up: An indication that it is time to be quiet on set.

Loge: Seating area in traditional proscenium arch venues. Exact location varies according to the venue, but is usually a box position at the dress circle level.

Long-Form Improv: Performers create shows in which short scenes are often interrelated by story, characters, or themes.

Long-Form Shows: May take the form of an existing type of theater, for example a full-length play or musical.

Long-Form Television: A miniseries that tells a story, usually an epic drama, with a limited number of episodes.

Long Lens: A lens which creates shallow focus, reduces the number of degrees visible, creates larger image size, and slows inward and outward movement.

Long Shot (LS): A shot that is still dominated by the environment, but the character becomes more of a focus than in an extreme long shot. *(Also known as Wide Shot)*

Look: The appearance of a show.

Look of Outward Regard: When an actor suddenly looks at something outside of the shot, which a viewer expects to then see what is there.

Look-See: A general interview.

Loop Film: A film with ends joined, creating a loop that can be run continuously through a projector.

Looping: Used in post-production to correct dialogue that has already been shot by re-recording the dialogue. Or, the art of matching lip movements and vitality of action in a scene. Or, use of audio/music on the loop. *(Also known as Dub or Dubbing)*

LORT: *See League Of Resident Theatres.*

Lot: The real estate occupied by a movie, television, or multimedia studio, which includes administrative offices and production facilities.

Low-Angle Shot: A shot taken from below a subject, creating a sense of looking up to whatever is photographed.

Low-Key: When light provides dim lighting, usually with heavy, dark shadows.

LS: Abbreviation for Left Stage. *(See Appendix: STAGE DIRECTION ABBREVIATIONS)*

Lucidity: Perfect clarity of adjustments.

Luminaire: A light. *(Also known as an Instrument or Lantern)*

Lunch: The meal served halfway through the shooting schedule, day or night.

LX: Abbreviation for Lighting.

Lyrics: The words to a song.

Lyric Sheet: A printed copy of the lyrics to a song.

Lyricist: The writer of the words to a song.

M

Maestro: The leader of the orchestra. *(Also known as Conductor)*

Magic Hour. The time of day when the sun casts a light which DP's have referred to as magic.

Magic If: Acting tool invented by Konstantin Stanislavski where the actor asks, "What would I do if I were the character in the situation?" The ability to honestly place oneself in the situation and circumstances of a character through the use of emotional recall, sense memory, and imagination. *(Also known as What If)*

Mahl Stick: A short stick used by scenic painters to steady the hand by resting its padded end against the surface being painted.

Main Rag: The front, often decorative, curtain of a stage.

Main Stage: The principal performance space for a theater company.

Major Meanings: The passions of a character that have the greatest significance in their life. The meanings are what give a character three dimensions and make up the core purpose of a character. It is the driving force that motivates their actions through each moment and compels them to achieve their super objective. For Romeo and Juliet, their major meanings are sexual love, family honor, and peer respect for Romeo, and married love, pleasing family, and religion for Juliet. *(Also known as Three Major Meanings)*

Make Fast: To tie off, in order to secure a flat, curtain, or other stage object.

Makeup: Cosmetics and sometimes hairstyles that an actor wears on stage to emphasize facial features, historical periods, characterizations, etc.

Makeup Designer: One who designs and applies makeup to actors in order to appear properly under stage lighting, or to appear older, younger, as a creature, etc.

Making an Entrance: The act of walking onto the stage in view of the audience. Or, doing something to be noticed coming into a space.

Making Your Points: Specifically and clearly communicating your needs or argument.

Manager: One who guides an artist in the development of their career.

Manet, Manent: A stage direction calling for a person, or more than one person, to remain on stage as others exit.

Mannerisms: Gestures, facial expressions, and vocal tricks that a particular actor uses again and again in different roles.

Manuscript: The written, or tangible version of the story. *(Also known as Script)*

Marionette: A puppet controlled by strings.

Mark: A designated position where an actor has to stand in order to be at a perfect angle for the shot.

Marker: A command used along with a slate board to indicate a visual cue for the camera.

Mark It: To signal the use of a slate board.

Marking Out: Marking the stage to indicate where everything will be placed.

Marking the Moment: When a scene has been created that is a significant moment in the drama, it is highlighted in some way.

Maroon: An electrically fired thunder flash, set off in a steel tank fitted with a wire mesh top, to simulate an explosion.

Marquee: A canopy or roof that projects over a theater entrance towards the street, usually bearing a sign that advertises the names of the theater, current production, actors, etc. Now, often used to mean only the sign.

Martini: The last shot of the day. *(Also known as Window)*

Mask: To block another actor. Or, a covering worn over the face or part of the face of an actor to emphasize or neutralize facial characteristics. Or, the fabric hiding a row of lanterns hung above the stage.

Masking: Drapery or flats used to frame the stage, and stop the audience from seeing the backstage areas.

Masks of Comedy and Tragedy: The masks that have come to signify "theater" represent two of the nine Greek muses. Comedy is represented by Melpomene [mel-po-men-ee] and tragedy by Thalia [thay-lee-a].

Master: The original recording.

Master Gesture: A distinctive action that is repeated and serves as a clue to a character's personality, such as a peculiar laugh or walk.

Master/Mistress of Ceremonies (MC): The person who announces the various parts of a program. *(Also known as Emcee)*

Master Shot: A single, uninterrupted shot of a scene which may be the only shot, or edited together with additional shots including multiple shot types.

Match Cut: A cut intended to blend two shots together unobtrusively.

Matching: Matching the look from one take or scene to exactly the same as in previous takes or scenes. Or, when one thing can be cut to another without disruption.

Matching Actions: When an actor has to match their previous actions for another shot after they have been established.

Matinee: A performance or showing that takes place in the afternoon.

Matinee Idol: A hugely popular movie star.

Matte Shot: A process for combining two separate shots on one print, resulting in a picture that looks as if it was photographed all at once.

Maximum Use Period: The length of time that holding fees must be paid when an actor shoots a commercial.

MC: *See Emcee or Master/Mistress of Ceremonies.*

MD: *See Musical Director.*

Meal Penalty: A payment to actors and extras if the production doesn't break for meals at least every six hours.

Mechanical Royalties. Money earned for use of a copyright in mechanical reproductions, most notably in music.

Medium Close-Up Shot: Falls between a medium shot and a close-up, generally framing the actor from chest or shoulder up.

Medium Long Shot (MLS): Between a full shot and a medium shot, this one usually shows the actor from the knees up, sometimes referred to as a 3/4 shot.

Medium Shot (MS): The most common shot used in the industry, shot from the waist up, it focuses on the actor while still showing some environment.

Medium Two Shot : This camera shot frames two people in a medium shot and can be expanded to a medium three shot, four shot, etc.

Megastar: Someone who is extremely famous. *(Also known as Superstar)*

Meisner Technique: An acting program that uses repetitive and in-the-moment exercises first devised by Sanford Meisner of the Group Theater. The technique emphasizes moment-to-moment spontaneity through communication with other actors to generate behavior that is truthful under imaginary circumstances.

Melodrama: A dramatic form popular in the 1800s and characterized by an emphasis on plot and physical action versus characterization, cliff-hanging events, heart-tugging emotional appeals, the celebration of virtue, and a strongly moralistic tone.

Melpomeme: The muse of tragedy, one of the nine muses of Mount Parnassus, believed by the Greeks to inspire those working in the arts or sciences.

Memory Play: A play where past events, as the protagonist recalls them, become the principal portions of the action.

Merde: The equivalent of Break a Leg, to wish someone a good performance.

Message: What the play as a piece of art is trying to say to the audience.

Method, Method Acting: The acting philosophy of using personal emotional experiences in acting, as first introduced to the western world by Konstantin Stanislavski and furthered by members of America's Group Theater in the 1930s. When used today, Method most often refers to the deeply personal emotional work taught by followers of Lee Strasberg, one of the Group Theater members, and can be summed up as training the subconscious to behave spontaneously.

Method Actor: An actor who becomes the character.

Metrics: The particular choice and order of objectives, activities, and adjustments in a script.

Metteur-En-Scene: A director or filmmaker, often used to indicate a director who does not deserve the title Auteur.

Mezzanine: In some theaters, a shallow gallery level above the main seating. *(Also known as Dress Circle or Royal Circle)*

Mic: Short for microphone, a recording device that transmits sound from the artist elsewhere. *(Also known as Microphone)*

Mic Drop: Literally, the gesture of intentionally dropping a microphone at the end of a performance or speech to signal triumph. Figuratively, it is an expression of triumph for a successful event, and indicates a boastful attitude toward one's own performance. *(Also known as Drop the Mic)*

Microphone: Usually referred to as mic, a recording device that transmits sound from the artist to someplace else. An omnidirectional mic has equal pick-up from all around, a cardioid mic is more sensitive from the front, a hypercardioid mic has very strong directionality from the front, and a figure-of-eight mic picks up front and rear, but rejects sound from the sides. *(Also known as Mic)*

Milk, Milking It: To draw the maximum response from the audience from comic lines or action.

Mime: An art form based on pantomime where conventionalized gestures are used to express ideas rather than words. Or, a performer of pantomime.

Mimesis: The Greek word meaning imitation, the term is used in criticism when discussing Aristotle's theory of imitation, or the creative process.

Mimic, Mimicry: An actor's ability to sound and/or look like someone else, usually a famous person.

Miming: Acting out, without words.

A Minor Consideration (AMC): An organization addressing the concerns of children in the industry. *(See   Appendix: ENTERTAINMENT INDUSTRY ASSOCIATIONS/ORGANIZATIONS)*

Mirror Ball: Lighting effect popular in ballrooms and other dance halls. A large plastic ball, usually motorized to rotate, covered with small mirror pieces. When a spotlight is focused onto the ball, specks of light are thrown around the room.

Mise-en-Scene: The aura emanating from details of setting, scenery, and staging.

Mistress/Master of Ceremonies (MC): The person who announces the various parts of a program.

Mit Out Sound (MOS): Slang for a shot taken without any sound or dialogue, attributed to the theory that a 1920s director with a heavy German accent pronounced it, "mit out sound." *(Also known as Motion Only Shot or Motor Only Shot or Motor Only Sync or Silent on Camera)*

Mix: The final audio product combining all the elements into one composite soundtrack.

Mixdown: Creating the mix.

Mixer: The person in charge of the sound crew, responsible for the quality of the sound.

Mixing Desk: Control desk for sound effects being used.

Mix Position: A location in the theater where a sound mixing console is operated during the performance.

Mockumentary, Mocumentary: A fictional, farcical film that has the style, look and feel of a documentary, with irreverent humor, parody, or slapstick, that is deliberately designed to mock the documentary or subject that it features.

Model: A scale model provided by the set designer to help all the technical departments to co-ordinate and plan a production. Used as a reference when building, painting, dressing and lighting the set.

Model Zed Card: A series of photographs, printed on a two or four sided card used for securing modeling work.

Modulate: To change from one key to another in a song.

Moment-to-Moment: The acting process concentrating on the present, not what's going to happen in the future.

Money Shot: A crucial or climactic moment, especially in a movie.

Monitor: The person in charge of checking actors in, giving them sides and deciding the order they will read. Or, an onstage speaker allowing a performer to hear the output of the PA system. Or, a display screen.

Monologue: An uninterrupted speech by a character in a performance or audition.

Montage: A method of putting shots together in such a way to make a statement or advance the story.

Mood: Emotional tone of the performance.

Moral: What the play as a piece of art is trying to convey to the audience.

MOS: *See Mit Out Sound or Motion Only Shot or Motor Only Shot.*

Motif: The shortest significant melody of a song or theme. Or, recurring structures, contrasts, or literary devices that can help to develop the major themes.

Motion Only Shot (MOS): A shot taken without any sound or dialogue, many times referred to as "mit out sound," attributed to one theory that a 1920s director with a heavy German accent pronounced it that way. *(Also known as Mit Out Sound or Motor Only Shot or Motor Only Sync or Silent on Camera)*

Motion Picture: A series of still images which, when shown on a screen, creates the illusion of moving images. Or, to capture on film as part of a series of moving images as in make a movie of a story or event. *(Also known as Film or Movie or Photoplay or Theatrical Film)*

Motion Picture & Television Fund (MPTF): An organization that supports the entertainment community in living and aging well, with dignity and purpose, and in helping each other in times of need. *(See Appendix: ENTERTAINMENT INDUSTRY ASSOCIATIONS/ORGANIZATIONS)*

Motion Picture Association of America (MPAA): An organization considered the voice and advocate of the American motion picture industry. *(See Appendix: ENTERTAINMENT INDUSTRY ASSOCIATIONS/ORGANIZATIONS)*

Motivating Drive: A character's pursuit of a specific goal in a scene. *(Also known as Actions or Driving Question or Essential Action or Intention or Objective)*

Motivation: The reason a character pursues a particular objective or super objective.

Motor Only Shot, Motor Only Sync (MOS): A shot taken without any sound or dialogue, many times referred to as "mit out sound," attributed to one theory that a 1920s director with a heavy German accent pronounced it that way. *(Also known as Mit Out Sound or Motion Only Shot or Silent on Camera)*

Mouth Noise: A dry mouth produces much more mouth noise than a damp one. The less mouth noise, the less editing has to be done later. *(Also known as Clicks and Pops)*

Movie: A series of still images which, when shown on a screen, creates the illusion of moving images. Or, to capture on film as part of a series of moving images as in make a movie of a story or event. *(Also known as Film or Motion Picture or Photoplay or Theatrical Film)*

Movie Star: A famous or popular movie actor.

Moving On: Going to the next scene.

Moviola: A projection machine that reduces film to a small viewing screen.

MPAA: *See Motion Picture Association of America.*

MPTF: *See Motion Picture & Television Fund.*

Mr. Nice Guy: In improv, a good improv player that makes it easy for other players to perform with them.

Mr. Sands: Theatrical code to warn theater employees of a fire without frightening the audience.

Mug, Mugging: To make exaggerated facial gestures in order to draw the audience's attention. Or, to strike a pose for a photographer.

Multicam, Multi-Camera: A method of filmmaking and video production where several cameras are used on the set and simultaneously record or broadcast a scene.

Multimedia: The combined use of several media, including sound, video, and text, to express ideas in communication, entertainment, or art.

Multiple Camera Show: When several cameras are simultaneously running, such as what is used for soap operas.

Mummer: An actor in a play without words.

Muse: Thalia is the Muse of Comedy and Melpomene is the Muse of Tragedy. Muses were minor Greek gods who were thought to inspire artistic endeavors and now refers to anyone who inspires another.

Music: All patterned sound, an important ingredient in every production.

Musical: A performance that emphasizes music as well as dance.

Musical Director: Responsible for the musical effects of the show, usually works with the director and orchestra.

Musical Revue: A production consisting of a series of independent songs.

Music Editor: Works with the composer and prepares the recordings from the scoring session for use in the final mix.

Music Hall: A vaudeville or variety theater, where performers take turns in entertaining an audience.

Music Publisher: The individual or company that screens songs and gets them commercially recorded, protects the copyrights, and collects income from performance, mechanical synchronization and printing rights, both in the United States and in foreign countries.

Music Under: Slang for background music.

Must Join: The 30-day grace period after being hired for a union job that an actor must join that union as mandated by the Taft-Hartley law.

N

Name Talent Only: Refers to areas that only principal actors can use.

Naming: Identifying characters, objects, places and so forth in the scene.

Narrator: A character who speaks directly to the audience.

National: A commercial airing everywhere in the US.

National Endowment for the Arts (NEA): Established by Congress in 1965 to support artistic excellence, creativity, and innovation through partnerships with state arts agencies, local leaders, other federal agencies, and the philanthropic sector. *(See Appendix: ENTERTAINMENT INDUSTRY ASSOCIATIONS/ORGANIZATIONS)*

Naturalism: Attempting to depict life and society as it is. Usually used to describe a play in its entirety, but also the individual work of a director or actor. *(Also known as Realism)*

ND Meal: Short for a non-deductible meal, which is a 15-minute meal break provided to actors by the production company to bring actors in sync with crew break time. It must be completed within 2 hours of performers' call time. *(Also known as Non-Deductible Meal)*

NEA: *See National Endowment for the Arts.*

Nearby Location: Any shooting location within a 30-mile radius of the studio.

Negative Cutting, Negative Matching: Cutting motion picture negative to match precisely the final edit as specified by the film editor.

Neoclassicism: Drama imitative of Greek and Roman classical models.

Neorealism: A film style using documentary techniques for fictional purposes.

Neutral Demo: A demo that doesn't sound like it is for one particular artist, but best represents the song, so that it can be recorded by anybody.

Never Ending Story: A scene that continues to introduce so many new ideas that it becomes impossible to tie the story together.

New Deal: Moving on to the next scene.

NewFilmmakers Los Angeles (NFMLA): A non-profit organization championing independent filmmakers worldwide. The festival provides a forum where filmmakers can be recognized for their accomplishments, gain exposure to new audiences, and connect with industry professionals for insight on distribution, production, acquisition, and representation. *(See Appendix: ENTERTAINMENT INDUSTRY ASSOCIATIONS/ORGANIZATIONS)*

NFMLA: *See NewFilmmakers Los Angeles.*

Night Premium: Additional pay for working past 8 p.m.

Night Shot: A scene specified in the script to be filmed when it is dark out.

Noddy Shot: This shot is used in recorded news or interviews to show the interviewer nodding or exhibiting other similar listening gestures.

Noh: One of the traditional forms of Japanese theater where masked male actors use highly stylized dance and poetry.

Noises Off: Offstage sound effects, such as a car crash, breaking glass, etc.

Non-Air: Something that is being produced as a test, but will not be aired.

Non-Deductible Meal: A 15-minute meal break provided to actors by the production company to bring actors in sync with crew break time. It must be completed within 2 hours of performers' call time. *(Also known as ND Meal)*

Non-Diegetic: Sound that cannot be heard by the characters, but is designed for the audience reaction.

Non-Linear Editing: Putting scenes together on a computer using film editing software capable of moving them around.

Non-Professional: Amateur theater or performer.

Nonsynchronous Sound: Sound that combines sounds from one source with visuals from another, such as the sound of an argument between two people with only one person walking alone visible, or the sounds of an alarm clock accompanying visuals of someone watching television or multimedia.

Non-Traditional Casting: When characters for a performed work are cast without regard to race, gender, age, etc., or cast against what is specified. (i.e., an adult plays a child, an African American actor plays a part previously only played by Caucasian actors, a woman plays a previously male role, etc.). *(Also known as Color-Blind Casting)*

Non-Union: A project or actor that is not affiliated with or does not belong to an actors union.

Notes: Instructions, usually regarding changes in an actor's blocking or performance, given after a rehearsal by the director, musical director, choreographer or stage manager.

Number: A song or dance in a musical production, so called because each musical selection is numbered for the convenience of the orchestra.

Number 1 Bar: The lighting bar immediately behind the proscenium arch or the front bar which hangs over the stage in a non-proscenium arch theater.

Nut: The actual or estimated cost of producing a show, often figured on a weekly basis.

O

OB: Slang terminology used to describe stage left when there is a bastard prompt corner. Stage right is then known as Bastard.

Object: Physical item used by the actor to enhance and give more reality to a character.

Objective: A character's pursuit of a specific goal in a scene. *(Also known as Driving Questions or Essential Action or Intention or Motivating Drive)*

Objective Acting: Use of learned skills of acting, movement, speech, and interpretation to create roles where no emotional response is used and performance is based on technique. *(Also known as Technical Acting)*

Objective Camera: A camera technique which conveys motionless detachment, such as from an invisible onlooker.

Oblique-Angle Shot: The camera is turned on its axis to the left or right for the shot to appear diagonally, as if tilting your head.

Obstacle: The conflict and stumbling blocks to a character's struggle in pursuit of an action or objective.

OC: *See Off Camera.*

Oeuvre: The collective body of work of an Auteur.

Off: A scene starting with a shot of one actor and opening to the scene. Or, a cue to an actor to take their cue off of the reaction of another actor.

Off Book: The term that refers for when actors must have all their lines memorized.

Off Broadway: New York City theaters that aren't located on Broadway or professional theaters with 100 to 499 seats, or a professional theater production that takes place outside New York City.

Off Camera: A dialogue or monologue performed by an actor who isn't in the shot.

Off Card: A union actor working on a non-union project.

Offer: Any dialog or action which advances the scene.

Offer from Space: Dialog or action that is bizarre and that appears to come from nowhere.

Office Scene: A two person script performed in the office of a producer, casting director, etc.

Off Off Broadway: Designates professional theaters with less than 100 seats, or is sometimes applied to any show in the New York City area that employs union actors but is not under an Off-Broadway, Broadway, or League of Resident Theatres contract.

Off Screen (O.S.): Used when the character is in the scene location and the voice is heard, but they are out of the camera's view so not currently on screen. *(Also known as Off Screen Voice)*

Off Screen Voice (OSV): Used when the character is in the scene location and the voice is heard, but they are out of the camera's view so not on screen. *(Also known as Off Screen)*

Offstage: Stage area that the audience cannot see.

Omnes, Omnies: Direction for the cast to make sounds as a group.

On: On the visible stage. Or, to be performing.

On a Bell: When the set is locked down during shooting.

On Avail: The casting director calls the agent or manager to ask if the actor is available for the specified shoot dates. The director then makes note of that availability and informs the person deciding who to cast.

On Book: When actors are still using scripts in rehearsals.

On Broadway: On-Broadway productions are staged in New York City's official theater district, between Sixth to Eighth Avenues and 41st to 54th Streets, and usually have 500 or more seats.

On Camera: A part in a television or multimedia spot, or video production where the actor actually appears on screen.

One: The first position for the scene.

One for Safety: The director may call for one extra take in case some unseen technical variable renders the good take useless. *(Also known as Insurance or Protection or Safety)*

One-Liner: A short version of the shooting schedule. Or, a one-line joke.

One Sheet: A single document that summarizes a product for publicity and sales.

One-Shot Feature Film: A full-length movie filmed in one long take by a single camera, or manufactured to give the impression it was. *(Also known as Continuous Shot Feature Film)*

On Hold: When an actor is contracted to be available for the next day's shoot, but will not have to report to the set until called. Or, when an actor is not scheduled to work, but must be available in case they are needed.

On Location: Working away from the sound stage or away from the home city.

Onomatopoeia: Use of words whose sounds echo their meanings.

On-or-About: A date which implies three different days, giving production twenty-four hours before and after the on-or-about date to start an actor.

On Spec, On Speculation: Definition: A script that is written and submitted without a contract or agreement in place.

Onstage: On the visible stage.

On the Floor: A slang term for being edited out of a final product. *(Also known as Cutting Room Floor)*

OP: *See Opposite Prompt.*

Open: The start of the run of a show in a venue. Or, the act that starts the show.

Open Audition. Audition that is open to the public.

Open Call, Open Casting Call: Same as cattle call where long days of general auditions are available for anybody.

Opening: The start of a performance.

Opening Credits: Credits shown in the beginning of a film or a television or multimedia show.

Opening Night: The first performance of a production. *(Also known as First Night)*

Opening Out: Angling or squaring the body out toward the audience or camera, while still partly facing the other actor. *(Also known as Cheating)*

Opening Up: An actor turning away from the audience.

Opening Sequence: The method by which films, television or multimedia programs present their title, key production and cast members, using conceptual visuals and sound.

Open the House: Clearance given to the front of house staff by stage management that the stage is set and the audience can begin to take their seats.

Open White (o/w): Lighting with no color filter.

Opera: Musical theater where all conversations are sung.

Opera Box: A seating area in a theater, usually with 2-12 loose instead of fixed chairs, and separated from adjacent areas by railings or half walls. *(Also known as Box)*

Operative Words: The primary words used within a sentence to communicate intended information.

Operetta: A form of musical theater where the music is lighter than opera.

Opposite Bastard (OB): Slang terminology used to describe stage left when there is a bastard prompt corner. Stage right is then known as Bastard.

Opposite Prompt (OP): The right hand side of the stage as you face the audience.

Opposition: When a performer chooses to make performance choices that are opposite what might be expected. Or, when a performer uses opposite tactics against one another to heighten a specific moment, such as to attack immediately following flattery.

Option: Acquiring the rights to a story for a certain amount of time that guarantees no one else can use that story.

Orchestra: The seats on the lower part of the theater. Or, the musicians that play during the show.

Orchestra Pit: A sunken area of the theater in the front of house where the conductor and musicians are seated.

Orchestration: The use of beats, builds, climax, change motion, and/or resolution within a piece that give the performance things that effect rhythm, intensity, and direction. *(Also known as Shaping)*

Organic: A natural response that comes from deep within the actor proceeding naturally from what has been presented.

OS: *See Off Stage.*

Oscars: An annual American awards ceremony hosted by the Academy of Motion Picture Arts and Sciences (AMPAS) to recognize excellence in cinematic achievements in the United States film industry as assessed by the Academy's voting membership. *(Also known as the Academy Awards)*

OT: *See Overtime.*

OTT: *See Over The Top.*

Out: In flying, means up out of sight. Or, in lighting, means turn off or dim completely.

Outcome: What happens after the character achieves their objectives.

Outer Tactics: The method of how an actor goes about doing their action in a beat, always preceded with by, and always ending in -ing. Each beat has both an inner action and an outer tactic, such as to gain money (inner action) by stealing (outer tactic).

Out of Frame: A performer that is outside of the camera's field of vision.

Outline: An idea or abridged script, containing a summary of each major scene and descriptions of the significant characters, usually one to ten pages. *(Also known as Treatment)*

Outrigger: An extendible leg to increase the stability of access equipment, such as a cherry picker lift or ladder.

Out Takes: Parts of an original filming or taping that will not be used in editing the finished product, unless an out-take segment is used for humor following the show.

Out Time: The time the actor leaves the set after changing out of their costume and removing makeup, etc.

Ovation: The positive response to a performance, usually marked by applause.

Overall Objective: What the character wants to accomplish throughout the entire play or film.

Overdub, Overdubbing: The addition of instruments or voices to pre-existing tracks.

Overlap: To speak when someone else is speaking.

Overloading: Throwing unnecessary elements into a scene, which usually leads to sidetracking. The introduction of a new and unnecessary character, which will usually prevent whatever was going to happen from happening.

Overnight Location: A shooting location where the actor must remain overnight.

Overplay: To overact.

Over the Shoulder (OS, O/S, OVS, X/S): A camera shot of the scene shot from behind or over the shoulder of an actor, revealing what they are seeing from their point of view.

Over The Top (OTT): Over-exaggerating when acting.

Overtime (OT): Work extending beyond the contractual workday.

Overture: The introductory music during a musical show to give the audience a feeling of what's to come.

P

PA: *See Production Assistant.*

PA: *See Public Address System.*

Pace: The speed the actor picks up their cue and delivers the next line of dialogue. Or, the speed that creates a style for the piece.

Pacing: The tempo of an entire performance.

Packager: One who selects and combines talent for shows.

Packed House: A full audience, with very few or no seats/room left.

Pan: A very bad review from a critic. Or, a sweeping camera shot/movement that goes from one end to the other without any cuts.

P&R: Abbreviation for Picture (headshot) and Resume.

Panning Shot, Panoramic Shot: Movement of the camera from left to right or right to left around an imaginary vertical axis.

Pantomime: Being silent, yet appearing to talk, such as a pretend speech when extras in the background are imitating real conversations.

Pants Role: A role depicting a young man or boy, but performed by a woman. *(Also known as Trouser Role)*

Paper: Complimentary tickets.

Paper the House: Giving away tickets to get the seats filled for a particular performance.

Parallel: The folding frame that forms the base of a readily portable platform.

Paraphrasing: Restating the lines of dialogue in one's own words.

Parascenium: In a Greek theater, the wall on either side of the stage, reaching from the back wall to the orchestra.

Parent Union: The first professional union you join. Subsequent unions are sister unions.

Parody: A humorous imitation of another work or genre.

Part: A character. Or, the portion of the script intended for one character.

Parterre: The upper part of the main seating, usually behind a cross aisle, and almost always steeper than the lower orchestra.

Particularization: The process Uta Hagen taught, making each event, person and place, down to the smallest physical object, as exact as possible. These details are explored in great detail to discover how they are relevant to the character.

Pathos: Strong exaggerated emotion.

Patron: A supporter of the theater, especially a paying member of the audience.

Patter: A set of amusing lines, rapidly spoken or sung by an actor. Also, the words for such lines.

Pause: A lull or a stop in dialogue or action in order to sustain emotion.

Pausing For Effect: A deliberate pause within or between lines used by an actor to call special attention to a moment.

Payola: A secret or private payment in return for the promotion of a product, service, etc., through the abuse of one's position, influence, or facilities. *(Also known as Plugola)*

Pay-or-Play: When an actor, director, or writer gets paid whether or not the project is made.

Pay-per-Airing: Money paid to an actor each time a television or multimedia commercial is shown.

Pay-to-Play: When the entertainer is responsible for some or all of the costs related to the show and the venue owner pays the rest. The owner then divides the profits with the entertainer in an agreed-upon split. Most pay-to-play comes in the form of two-walling or four-walling.

Peg: Slang for a clothespin used as props or to hang props. *(Also known as 47 or Ammo or Bullet or C-47 or CP47)*

Pen: To compose or write.

Perch: A place for hanging lanterns, on the side wall of the theater auditorium.

Per Diem: Money given to actors and crew when on location to cover the daily expense of food and other personal incidentals.

Perform, Performance: Providing entertainment for an audience.

Performance Royalties: Money earned from use of one's song on radio, television, multimedia, and other users of music.

Performers Work Report: Lists the names of all the performers who worked that day, including the time they arrived, went to makeup and wardrobe, were on set, started and ended their meal break and officially wrapped for the day. This time sheet is used to calculate the payment to the performer at the end of production's shooting schedule. *(Also known as Time Sheet)*

Performer: Someone who performs in front of an audience.

Performing Edition: The published text of a dramatic work, with alterations from the standard text to match the actualities of stage production, often including staging information.

Performing Right: Rights granted by US copyright law which states that one may not publicly perform a copyrighted work without the owner's permission.

Performing Rights Organization: Society whose purpose is to collect money earned from public performances of copyrighted work to distribute to the copyright owners in a proportion that reflects as accurately as possible the amount of performances of each particular song.

Period: Project not set in current time period.

Period Piece: A performance played in the style, costumes, and sets representing the period of time it depicts.

Persistence of Vision: A human characteristic which blends frames together for 1/10 of a second.

Personal Manager: The personal manager is an adviser that guides the client's professional choices. When working with a client that has yet to hit celebrity status, the personal manager may front money to the client for necessities like headshots, etc.

Personal Props: Props that actors carry with them.

Perspective: The way the object appears on screen in terms of relative position and distance.

Phone Patch: A session where the talent and the director are in separate locations. The session must be connected by phone so everyone can hear everyone else.

Photo Call: Some actors may need to appear in publicity photos for a show. This usually happens 2-3 weeks before opening and a photo call will be scheduled.

Photo Double: An actor, usually an extra, used in place of a principal actor, and only seen partially, and never has any speaking lines. *(Also known as Driving Double)*

Photoplay: A series of still images which, when shown on a screen, creates the illusion of moving images. Or, to capture on film as part of a series of moving images as in make a movie of a story or event. *(Also known as Film or Motion Picture or Movie or Theatrical Film)*

Psychic Action: The emotional growth or change of characters within the world of the production, but further verification is needed to make this determination.

Physical Film Producer: Once there is a script, director, cast and financing, this person oversees the entire production, including setting up a production company, etc., and then in post-production, helping to edit shot footage.

Physical Gesture: A specific movement or physical action of a character that expresses the psychology, feelings and desires incorporated into one gesture.

Physical Humor: Laughter evoked through exaggerated and outrageous behavior or the physical characteristics of a performer.

Physicalization: Turning intent into action and movement by expressing with showing as opposed to telling, the personality of a character, such as how they eat, walk, talk, etc.

Physical Separation: Moving two or more parts of the body in different dynamics simultaneously.

Piano Dress, Piano Rehearsal: Rehearsal in costume and with all technical facilities but using a piano as a substitute for the orchestra, so that the director can concentrate on technical problems.

Pick: A song that has been reviewed by the trades and projected to have success.

Picking Up Cues: Performers acting on their cues faster than they previously have.

Pick Up: Reshooting a section of a scene from a specific point. Or, to start reading the script from a place other than the beginning. Or, a request to read faster. Or, a way of describing the directional sensitivity of a microphone.

Pick-up Shot: Small parts of a scene that are re-shot, usually because all angles were not captured satisfactorily during the first shooting.

Picture: The video portion of a production.

Picture's Up: This line is shouted when a cue to shoot a scene is coming.

Piggy Back: A camera shot with both actors involved, facing the camera one behind the other, which allows both characters to have their private thoughts about each other, while allowing the audience to see what both characters are thinking/feeling.

Pig Iron: Cast iron weight placed to prevent movement of props. *(Also known as Brace Weight or Stage Weight)*

Pilot: A first episode of the television or multimedia show that is produced in order to sell the whole show.

Pilot Presentation: A one-day shoot that provides 7-10 minutes of edited video to give a network an idea of the look and feel of a proposed program.

Pilot Season: The time period when most television or multimedia shows are created, such as in California, where it's January-March.

Pimping: Playfully getting another performer to do something difficult or unpleasant which you probably wouldn't do yourself.

Pink Noise: Random sounding audio noise containing all frequencies in the audio spectrum tuned to the response of the human ear, used with a spectrum analyzer to set equalization equipment for a large PA installation.

Pin Spot: Either a small spotlight used for special effects, such as with a mirror ball, or to illuminate just a face.

Pipeline: A listing or schedule of movie projects in some stage of production.

Pipes: The bars on which scenery and instruments are flown.

Pirating: The unauthorized reproduction and selling of copyrighted work.

Pit: The sunken area in front of the stage where the orchestra sits.

Pitch: To audition or sell. Or, the position of a tone in a musical scale or the highness or lowness of a voice.

Pitching: The action a producer takes in trying to convince a studio to invest money in a project based on a concept or a script.

Pit Net: Protective net across the orchestra pit to prevent any objects or actors falling from the stage and injuring musicians.

Places: A command for all actors to take their designated positions.

Plan: A scale drawing showing a piece of scenery, lighting layout, etc., from above.

Planted Spin Off: A television or multimedia movie or an episode of an existing series that is a setup for a television or multimedia series of its own if ratings warrant further production. *(Also known as Back Door Pilot)*

Plateau: A period during which a scene is not advancing.

Platform: The who, what and where of a scene.

Platinum Album/Single: Certification by the Recording Industry Association of America that an album/single has sold a minimum of one million units.

Play: The stage representation of an action or a story.

Playbill: A pamphlet, booklet or program that contains information about the show, including the actors' biographies. Or, a poster of the show.

Player: Performer.

Playing the Ending: When the actor is performing in relation to the ending of the scene or play instead of dealing with what is happening in the moment.

Playing the Positive: Using the most positive methods one can, under the given circumstances, to achieve one's goals. In the end, violence may become the only option left thus making it positive.

Playlist: In improv, the list of handles and/or ask-fors to be used in a show. *(Also known as Running Order)*

Playwright: A person who writes plays and dramatic literature, also known as dramatist.

Plot: To set the lighting.

Plot, Plot Line: The main events of a play, novel, movie, or similar work, devised and presented by the writer as an interrelated sequence. Or, to plan stage business, as to plot the action or to plan a speech by working out the phrasing, emphasis, and inflections.

Plough/Plow Monday: The Monday after Epiphany, or Twelfth Night, which is January 6. In sixteenth-century England, the plays performed on Plough Monday had characters that were not heroes like Robin Hood, but farm hands, and the chief incident was a death by accident.

Plug: Promotion of a product, service, performance, etc. Or, the broadcast of a song.

Plugola: A secret or private payment in return for the promotion of a product, service, etc., through the abuse of one's position, influence, or facilities. *(Also known as Payola)*

Plus Ten: The 10% commission negotiated by an agent, specifically referring to the 10% added to the base pay negotiated for the actor. If the job pays only scale, the agent cannot take a percentage unless he has negotiated the contract to be on a plus-ten basis.

Point Cue: A cue inserted during or after plotting between two existing cues.

Pointing Lines: Emphasizing an idea.

Point of Attack: The place in the story where the playwright begins the plot.

Point of Concentration: A character's pursuit of a specific goal in a scene.

Point of View (P.O.V.): Examination from a certain perspective.

Point of View Shot (POV): A shot that shows the scene through the character's eyes to see the world from their point of view.

Points: A percentage of money producers and artists earn on the retail list price of 90% of all music sold.

Point Up: To stress certain lines, movements, or gestures, by directing the attention of the audience to something of dramatic importance, as in order to create suspense.

Polar Attitudes: The emotional or psychological distance that is made from the beginning of a piece to the end by the growth or change that takes place.

Pop: Creating a puff of wind that slightly distorts the recording when you say P's or B's or other plosive letters into the mic. *(Also known as Popped or Popping)*

Pop Filter: A foam cover or fabric guard placed over a microphone to help prevent popped P's and other plosive sounds. *(Also known as Windscreen or Windsock)*

Popped, Popping: Sudden release of blocked air into a microphone causing a popping sound. *(Also known as Pop)*

Position: The orientation of the actor to the audience, such as full front, right profile, left profile, etc.

Post, Post Production: All the work that goes into a production after the talent leaves. This includes such processes as editing, adding special effects, etc.

Post-Show: Discussion of the show by the performers and crew after the performance, in order to identify problem areas as well as things that worked particularly well.

POV: *See Point of View.*

POV Shot: Point of view camera shot.

Practical Props, Practicals: Props that actually have to work during performance, such as a cigarette lighter, flashlight, lights in the ceiling, etc.

Pratfall: A performer's fall or stunt, with humorous exaggeration.

Preceding Circumstances: What has taken place in the world of the story immediately before the beginning of a scene or the entrance of a character, etc.

Preferred Reading: The interpretation of the script that is stressed by the author or the text itself.

Prelay: The advance preparation of sound elements such as sound effects, dialogue, etc.

Preliminary Situation: The story of the play as the curtain rises.

Prelude: Usually a short introduction that leads into an act without a break, as opposed to an overture which is longer and can be played as a separate piece.

Premis: The intellectual value of the script.

Prep: Getting ready to shoot a film.

Pre-Production: The stage that the production is in before all the filming begins, such as the writing, casting, location scouting, etc.

Prep Schedule: Everything planned during the week before shooting, such as meetings, flights, etc.

Pre-Read: A brief advance reading, many times by phone, for a casting director who is unfamiliar with an actor's work prior to an audition or taking the actor to meet a producer or director.

Pre-Release: Work that is not yet listed for licensing.

Pre-Screen: An audition that casting directors will ask for, so they can meet the actor and see what they can do.

Presence: An actor's ability to command attention on stage, even when surrounded by other actors.

Presence: The silence recorded at a location or space when no dialogue is spoken. *(Also known as Room Tone)*

Presentational: A style of acting and staging that relates directly to the audience, instead of attempting to represent actual life realistically in every detail.

Presenting: The results of the creating process, including performances and evaluation.

Preset: When a prop or costume is placed on the stage before the show begins.

Press: The media. Or, the manufacture of a large quantity of vinyl records duplicated from a master for commercial sale.

Press Kit: A printed or virtual presentation including newspaper clippings, review of movie, television, multimedia, musical and theater productions, a biography, headshot, and resume, given to the media and interested industry professionals. *(Also known as Press Package)*

Press Opening: A special performance before opening night where members of the press are invited. Usually, critics are invited for opening night.

Press Package: A printed or virtual presentation including newspaper clippings, review of movie, television, multimedia, musical and theater productions, a biography, headshot, and resume, given to the media and interested industry professionals. *(Also known as Press Kit)*

Preview: A performance with an audience before official opening night, usually for just friends and family.

Preview: The advertisement for a film. *(Also known as Trailer)*

Prima Donna: Meaning first lady, the leading woman singer in an opera. Or someone who acts in a superior or demanding fashion. The term for the leading man is Primo Duomo.

Primary: A large movement.

Primary Source: The individual whose posture, movements, habits, voice inflections, and mannerisms are observed in order to build character.

Principal: Any role with lines or with significant importance to the storyline.

Principal Photography: The main shooting period of a film.

Principal Player: An actor with lines, paid at least SAG-AFTRA scale (minimum).

Print: Director's cue that the shot was good enough to use.

Printed Edition: A song published in the form of sheet music.

Print It: What the director tells the script supervisor when he or she wants a shot to appear on the dailies, and may also signal that work on a shot is done, though not always.

Private Moment: A well-known technique developed by Lee Strasberg, based on Konstantin Stanislavski's theory that the challenge of the actor is to act privately in public.

Process: Specific techniques, methods and tools that an actor uses to be able to live truthfully in an imaginary circumstance. *(Also known as Acting Process)*

Process Shot: A shot which joins foreground and background action which was filmed separately.

Producer: The person responsible for the business side, as well as financing and supervising, who oversees the making of a production from inception to completion.

Production: The show, play, or movie. Or, the technical aspects of the industry.

Production Assistant: The person responsible for a wide variety of things during a film production. *(Also known as Gofer or Runner)*

Production Carpenter: The one in charge of the backstage crew, even though working with wood may not be involved.

Production Company: The firm that is backing the production.

Production Designer: Develops the look for the film, such as costumes, set, props, etc. *(Also known as Art Director)*

Production Desk: Table in the auditorium at which the director/designer, etc., sit during rehearsals.

Production Draft: A shooting script that is still changing indicates changes on a page by a new page color. A production shooting script indicates changes by a new page or text color, or the color name written on the top of the page According to the WGA west, the standard script revision color sets are: White (unrevised), Blue, Pink, Yellow, Green, Goldenrod*, Buff, Salmon, Cherry, Second Blue Revision (also known as double blue), Second Pink Revision (aka double pink), and so on.... *Most scripts never make it past goldenrod. *(Also known as Production Script)*

Production Manager: Responsible for technical preparations, including budgeting and scheduling.

Production Script: A shooting script that is still changing indicates changes on a page by a new page color. A production shooting script indicates changes by a new page or text color, or the color name written on the top of the page According to the WGA west, the standard script revision color sets are: White (unrevised), Blue, Pink, Yellow, Green, Goldenrod*, Buff, Salmon, Cherry, Second Blue Revision (also known as double blue), Second Pink Revision (aka double pink), and so on.... *Most scripts never make it past goldenrod. *(Also known as Production Draft)*

Production Sound Mixer: Responsible for all sound recording on the set during the production. *(Also known as Location Sound Engineer or Sound Mixer)*

Production Title: The temporary title of a project used during its development. *(Also known as Working Title)*

Production Track: The sound recorded when the show was shot.

Professional: Normally used for someone who's regularly paid for a particular job, as opposed to an amateur, who does it for no pay.

Professional Comps: Complimentary tickets for agents, directors or casting directors.

Professional Manager: The person in charge of screening new material for a production company.

Professional Release: A play licensed only to professional companies.

Professional Rights, Professional Royalty: A professional company is one that pays a salary to actors, directors, designers and other staff, whether or not the company is profit or not-for-profit. Rights for professional companies are normally based on a percentage of the gross, typically 8-10% of the gross box office receipts.

Profile: Light providing a hard-edged beam. Or, a performer's view from the side. Or, a shaped piece of scenery added to the edge of a flat instead of a straight edge.

Profile Spot: The most commonly used lighting instruments that feature a long light throw which creates a circular pool of light on the stage. *(Also known as Ellipsoidal or ER Spotlights or Leko)*

Program Director: Person who determines which show will be broadcast.

Program Syndication: The sale of programs directly to stations or cable channels.

Program Use: When a test commercial gets used as an actual commercial.

Project Developer: Write or supervise the writing of a screenplay that can attract a director, cast and financing.

Projection: An actor's ability to use his or her voice so that it can be clearly heard in the back rows of a theater. Also used in reference to the emotions an actor wishes to convey.

Project Packager: When a screenplay is finalized, the film must be packaged and financing secured. The film package consists of the script and the names of the director, producer, and cast, as well as a flexible budget and production schedule.

Prologue: The action before the entrance of the actors or chorus.

Promenade: A performance of a play where the actors and audience occupy the same space, with no distinction between acting area and audience area. The audience is given the freedom to explore the space together with the performance, and there is generally an element of audience interaction in the play.

Promoter: One who secures talent from an agent for the production and presentation of a performance.

Prompt: A person who attends off-book rehearsals and gives actors the lines when they forget and call for a line. *(Also known as Prompter)*

Promptbook: A copy of a script for the use of a prompter during a performance.

Prompt Copy: Master copy of the script with all moves and technical effects included.

Prompt Corner: Area, traditionally on the stage left side of the stage where the stage manager or ASM controls/prompts the performance, usually from the prompt desk. *(Also known Corner)*

Prompt Desk: Desk in the prompt corner where the stage manager or ASM controls/prompts the performance.

Prompter: A person who is charged with prompting. *(Also known as Prompt)*

Prompt Side: The left side of the stage, facing the audience.

Prop, Property: Small and sometimes hand-carried objects used by actors during performance, not including costumes.

Property: Any intellectual property in any form, including a script.

Prop Master/Mistress: In charge of all the props.

Propping: The task, usually performed by stage management, of going around finding/borrowing/buying props for the production.

Prop Table: Table in a convenient offstage area where props not being used at the moment are stored during a performance.

Pro-Rata: What the producer is actually paying per day.

Proscenium: The view of the stage for the audience. The boundary between the stage and the audience in a conventional theater which appears to form an arch over the stage from the audience's point of view.

Proscenium Arch Stage: The classic theater arrangement, with a curtained stage facing an audience on one side, which appears to form an arch over the stage from the audience's point of view.

Prose: Lines of varied length with no rhyme and no meter.

Prosody: The marriage of words and music.

Protagonist: The main character.

Protection: The additional take filmed, even though there is one that seems good enough, just in case. *(Also known as Insurance or One for Safety or Safety)*

PSA: *See Public Service Announcement.*

Pseudomonologue: When only one half of a dialogue is portrayed, especially either just the questions or the answers, wherein the performer is not directly addressing the audience.

Psychophysical Action: Purposeful action undertaken to fulfill a character's goals is the most direct route to emotions.

Psychological Gesture: A movement that has intention and expresses the psychology of the character.

Public Address System (PA): The venue sound system.

Publication: The printing and distribution of copies of a work to a public by sole or other transfer of ownership, or by rental, lease or lending.

Public Broadcasting System (PBS): Association of public television stations designed to facilitate the sharing of programs.

Public Domain: Unprotected by copyright due to an expired copyright or caused by an invalid copyright.

Publicist: A person hired to create awareness of a person or project, while running damage control against any bad news.

Public Service Announcement (PSA): A message aired on television, multimedia, or radio without charge, with the objective of raising awareness or changing public attitudes and behavior towards a social issue.

Publisher: A person or company that prepares and issues books, journals, music, or other works for sale.

Pull Back: The camera physically moves away from a subject, usually through a zoom or dolly action.

Pull Focus: The camera focus changes from one object or subject to another.

Pulling Focus: Improperly taking attention from an actor who should be the focus of interest.

Punchline: A line of dialogue that carries particular emphasis for dramatic or comic effect.

Puppetry: Almost anything brought to life by human hands to create a performance. Types of puppets include rod, hand, and marionette.

Purpose: A character's pursuit of a specific goal in a scene.

Push and Pull: Actors who move scenery/furniture around the stage, earning them extra money.

Push In: The camera physically moves towards a subject.

Pushing Cues: Eliminating the spaces between cues.

Pyropot: A safe container into which a pyrotechnics charge is plugged for firing.

Pyrotechnics: Chemical explosive or flammable firework effects.

Q

Q: Abbreviation for Cue, as in cue the talent.

Q Rating, Q Score: Refers to an ad research rating that gauges how easily a celebrity is recognized, and how well the celebrity is liked.

the Quarter: Announcements are sometimes made to the audience into the auditorium and front of house informing them when the performance will begin. Calls may be made at the Half (30 min. before curtain up), the Quarter (15 min), the Five (5 min), and normally accompanied by bar bells, usually at 2 minutes before the performance begins.

Query: A method of submission in which a writer sends someone a brief letter, sometimes accompanied by a synopsis and sample pages. Or, to ask a question about something.

Queued Up: Previewing a taped performance and having it set to start playing at specific moment.

Quick Study: An actor who can memorize lines quickly.

Quid Pro Quo: When a character or the audience mistakes someone or something for someone or something else.

Quiet on the Set: The prompt for everyone to be quiet for filming.

Quote: The amount that studios and casting directors keep of a performer's salary. Or, repeat a group of words from a text or speech, typically with an indication that one is not the original author or speaker. Or, giving or getting the estimated cost for a particular job or service.

R

R: Abbreviation for Right Stage. *(See Appendix: STAGE DIRECTION ABBREVIATIONS)*

Rack: A cabinet of 19" width into which various components can be bolted. Racks are ideal for touring equipment.

Rack Focus: A technique changing the focus from one subject to another within the same shot. *(Also known as Focus Through)*

Radio Mic: A microphone hidden in the actors clothes which broadcasts to a receiver nearby.

Rain Box: A box or tray containing dried peas, etc., which produces a rain sound effect when inclined.

Raising the Stakes: Making the events of the scene have greater consequences for the characters.

Raissoneur: Usually a supporting character who helps the audience keep track of the values of the story.

Rake, Raked Stage: A tilted performing area, usually specially constructed, with its upstage space raised slightly higher than the downstage space.

Ramp: A sloping platform on which an actor may walk. A ramp may lead up to the stage from the auditorium floor, from the stage floor to a platform, etc.

Range: The extent of an actor's ability to perform different types of roles. Or, the vocal extent of a singer's voice.

Raspberry: Slang for a jeer from the audience.

Rating: The percentage of all homes that are tuned to a particular network at a particular time.

Rave: An extremely good review from a critic.

R&B: Abbreviation for Rhythm & Blues music.

RC: Abbreviation for Right Center Stage. *(See Appendix: STAGE DIRECTION ABBREVIATIONS)*

RCS: Abbreviation for Right Center Stage. *(See Appendix: STAGE DIRECTION ABBREVIATIONS)*

Reaction Shot: The camera shooting a character's emotional or physical response or reaction to something.

Reader: Another actor who is paid, or volunteers, to help the casting office by playing all the other characters during an audition so the casting director can concentrate on the actor being screened.

Reader's Theater: Presentation of a play where the actors read from scripts, usually with no movement or staging.

Read for a Part: In auditions, to read one's lines aloud to a stage director or casting agent.

Reading, Read-Through: A first reading of a script by the cast that is going to perform on the show to get familiar with the story, their roles, and their fellow actors.

Realism: Attempting to depict life and society as it is. Usually used to describe a play in its entirety, but also the individual work of a director or actor. *(Also known as Naturalism)*

Rear of House (ROH): Area in the back of the stage, usually used to store props and furniture.

Recall: When a production company decides to use an actor's services for an additional day.

Recitative: Words sung in a conversational style, usually to advance the plot.

Recognition: The point in the plot at which a character understands his or her situation as it really is.

Recording Industry Association of America (RIAA): A trade organization that represents the recording industry in the United States, whose members consist of record labels and distributors. *(See Appendix: ENTERTAINMENT INDUSTRY ASSOCIATIONS/ORGANIZATIONS)*

Recurring Role: Typically found on television or multimedia shows where the character shows up from time to time in a few episodes of a series.

Reel: A video compilation of an actor's best work. *(Also known as Tape)*

Reestablishing Shots: Reminders or updates on scene changes where people have moved.

Regional: A commercial airing only in a certain part of the United States.

Regional Theater: Permanent nonprofit professional theater companies that have established roots outside the major theater centers. Besides bringing first-rate theater to their region, they often have programs to nurture local talent and to encourage new plays of special regional interest. *(Also known as Resident Theater)*

Rehearsal: Time of practice and blocking before the actual performance either on stage or in front of the camera.

Rehearse: To prepare for production, in particular, the work with actors to blend lines, characterization, movement and stage business into a coherent whole.

Reincorporation: Bringing back an idea from earlier in the scene, or from a previous scene in the show, or even from a previous performance. *(Also known as Call Back)*

Release: The issuing of a film to the public by a studio. Or, a legal document releasing someone from liability.

Remembered Emotion: Memory that involves the actor personally, so that deeply rooted emotional experiences can be relived in the performance. *(Also known as Affective Memory)*

Rental: Scripts normally are purchased, however in some cases, scripts are rented. The standard rental time is two months prior to your initial performance. Additional fees usually apply for each additional rental week.

Rep: Abbreviation for Representative.

Repertoire: Stock pieces that a singer or company has ready to present. Or, a company's current season.

Repertory Theater: A theater group that rehearses several plays at a time.

Representation: The act of, or the agent/agency or manager representing the interests of a performer professionally.

Representational: Represents realism, where characters in their real lives that are not aware the audience is there.

Representative: The individual or company representing the interests of the performer.

Reprise: Repeating the performance in whole or in part.

Reset: The actors and set should return to their positions and the way it was at the beginning of the scene. *(Also known as Back-to-One or From the Top or To Ones)*

Reshoot: Redoing a portion of a film after principal photography has ended.

Resident Theater: Permanent nonprofit professional theater companies that have established roots outside the major theater centers. Besides bringing first-rate theater to their region, they often have programs to nurture local talent. *(Also known as Regional Theater)*

Residual: A pay that performers, except extras, get every time the production they were a part of gets rebroadcast. *(Also known as Royalty)*

Resolution: The sorting out or unraveling of a plot at the end of a play, novel, or story.

Restricted: Performance rights to a play may not be available if a play is running on or off-Broadway, or is on national tour. Or a professional theater in your area may have secured rights to produce the play, barring all other local productions until its run has closed.

Resume: Usually attached to a headshot, this is a list of actor's information, including credits, personal details, special skills, etc. *(See Appendix: ACTOR'S RESUME)*

Retouching: A photographic process whereby certain flaws in a picture are covered up or removed.

Reversal: The point at which the action of the plot turns in an unexpected direction for the protagonist.

Reverse Angle Shot: A camera shot set up to shoot the reverse 180° view of the previous shot.

Reversibles: A costume that is double-faced so that by reversing it, the illusion of a different costume is created.

Revised Final: The final version of a script/screenplay.

Revised Pages: Changes are made to the script after the initial circulation of the production script, which are different in color and incorporated into the script without displacing or rearranging the original, unrevised pages.

Revolve, Revolving Stage: Stage which turns in a circle.

Revue: A series of songs, dances, and sketches, assembled to present a theme, but without a through storyline.

Rewrite: Editing a script. Or, change notifications in the script for performers using color coded pages.

Rhubarb: Background conversation by extras. So-called because extras were often asked to mutter the word "rhubarb" to produce the effect of genuine conversation, with their mouths moving convincingly.

RIAA: *See Recording Industry Association of America.*

the Rideout: The music that begins on the downbeat of the last word of the song.

Rider: An addition to a performer's union contract that outlives a special circumstance for pay. Or, information sent to a venue by a touring group detailing lighting, sound, staging, and dressing room requirements.

Rig: To set the lights in position. Or, the actual positioning of the lights.

Rigger: One who works on ropes, booms, lifts and other aspects of a production.

Rigging: Collectively, the ropes, wires, blocks, pulleys, pins, counterweights, and other pieces of equipment needed in the manipulation of scenery and stage drapery.

Right: Refers to the stage from an actor's point of view, not from that of the audience.

Right Frame: The side of the shot where the performers are kept from the camera operator's perspective. *(Also known as Camera Right)*

Rights: The author, via the representative or publisher, confers on a theater or production company the right to produce a production as set forth in the signed contract.

Right-to-Work: Ability to accept employment without joining a labor union, usually referring to states whose labor codes ensure that right.

Right-to-Work State: In a right-to-work state, actors who have not joined a union may do both union and nonunion work. Companies cannot refuse to hire an actor because they do not belong to a union or do not want to join a union. This does not mean that a union actor in one of these states may do both union and nonunion work; union actors must still abide by union rules.

Ring Up: To raise the curtain.

Riser: A platform on the stage that creates different levels.

Rising Action: The events of a dramatic or narrative plot preceding the climax, when a dramatic situation that contains a serious conflict has been created, and rising action begins and continues to build until the character finds a way to solve the conflict.

Ritual: A prescribed form or ceremony.

Roadie: Touring technician with shows on the road.

Road Manager: The person in charge of a touring cast when they are traveling to different performance locations. *(Also known as Company Manager)*

Road Show: A touring production.

Rockumentary: A documentary about rock music and musicians.

ROH: *See Rear of House.*

Role: The characteristic and expected social behavior of an individual in a given position.

Role Play: Exploring attitudes and beliefs.
Role Scoring: The analysis of a character.
Roll Camera: What the director says to signal the cameraman to begin filming. *(Also known as Turn Over)*
Roll Drop: Drops flown on rollers.
Rolling: Cameras have been turned on.
Roll It, Roll Over: A command then given to start rolling the cameras and sound, answered by the call speed when the production sound mixer is recording.
Romantic Comedy: A movie that has both romance and comedy.
Rom-Com: Slang for a romantic comedy.
Room Tone: The silence recorded at a location or space when no dialogue is spoken. *(Also known as Presence)*
Roster: A talent agents list of clients who they can submit for projects.
Rostra, Rostrum: Blocks or platforms used to create levels.
Rough Cut: The version of the film where the changes following the screenplay are made, as in the first draft of an edited version. *(Also known as Editor's Cut or First Assembly)*
Royal Circle: In some theaters, a shallow gallery level above the main seating. *(Also known as Dress Circle or Mezzanine)*
Royalty: Money earned from repeated use of a performance. *(Also known as Residual)*
Royalty House: Companies sell or rent scripts and scores and also license plays for production.
R&R: Abbreviation for Rock & Roll music.
RS: Abbreviation for Right Stage. *(See Appendix: STAGE DIRECTION ABBREVIATIONS)*
Run: A series of brief lines building to a speech or key moment. Or, the number of times that the stage show has been performed.
Run Italians: To speak one's lines very fast, either individually or as a cast to assist in committing lines and cues to memory.
Run Lines: Committing dialogue to memory, usually practicing out loud with someone else.
Runner: Employed as production assistant to do odd jobs and errands during a production period. *(Also known as Gofer or Production Assistant)*

Runners: A pair of curtains parting in the center and running horizontally, particularly those used in a downstage position in variety and revue productions.

Running Blacks: Full stage width black tabs with a split half way, which are usually fitted to a tab track so that they can be opened and closed horizontally and flown in and out.

Running Gag: Recycling a situation or character from a previously played scene.

Running Order: In improv, the list of handles and/or ask-fors to be used in a show. *(Also known as Playlist)*

Running Plot: A plot giving details of the changes between cues.

Running Time: The time it takes to run through the production, including intermissions.

Run-Through: Rehearsal where the whole show is being run from the beginning to the end.

Runway: A narrow projection of the stage, into the orchestra pit or into the aisle of the auditorium, on which a performer can walk.

Rush Call: A last minute call by an agency to an actor for an audition or a job.

Rushes: The raw unedited footage for the day delivered to the director for viewing to make sure the footage is satisfactory. *(Also known as Dailies)*

S

Safe Second: Stars from an underperforming television or multimedia series start booking pilots, but the pilot role is null and void should their current show be renewed. A safe second means the pilot's bosses have been assured the actor in question will be available.

Safety: The director may call for one extra take in case some unseen technical variable renders the good take useless. *(Also known as Insurance or One for Safety or Protection)*

Safety Chain: Chain or wire fixed around lantern and lighting bar or boom to prevent danger in the event of failure of the primary support.

Safety Curtain: A curtain of fireproofed material that covers the entire proscenium opening and acts as a firebreak between the stage and the auditorium. *(Also known as Iron)*

SAG-AFTRA: *See Screen Actors Guild.*

SAG-Eligible: A non-union actor who is eligible to join SAG-AFTRA by being cast in a principal role, being a member of an affiliated union and having had a principal role under that union's jurisdiction, or performing three days of union extra work.

SAG-Franchised: Status of an agent or agency that has signed papers with SAG.

Sampling: The technique of recording a sound digitally for subsequent processing, editing and playback.

Satire: A style of comedy that presents humorous attacks on accepted conventions of society.

Scale: Minimum daily wage for principal actors under union contracts.

Scale +10: Minimum payment + 10% to cover an agent's commission.

Scalper: Someone who buys scarce tickets to a popular production and resells them to the highest bidder.

Scenario: An outline of the plot.

Scene: Action taking place in one location and in a distinct time that moves the story to the next element of the story. Or, a portion of a script that has been given its own number.

Scene Dock: Backstage area for storing scenery.

Scene Heading: A short description of the location and time of day of a scene (e.g., EXT. CABIN - DAY). *(Also known as Slugline)*

Scenery: Resources used to create the setting where a production takes place, such as the furniture, etc.

Scene Shift: A movement of scenery by stagehands to change a stage setting between scenes.

Scene Shop: The area where scenery is built or repaired.

Scene Stealing: Improperly or inadvertently taking attention from an actor who should be the focus of interest.

Scene Study and Analysis: A class in breaking down scripts to discover what they really mean, character intentions, motivations and more to use as a pre-audition practice of studying a few pages of a script ahead of time. Or, to assist with performance preparation.

Scenic Charge: One who is responsible for the preparation scenery.

Scenic Paint: Traditionally, a mixture of glue, water and pigment. Modern practice has also adopted PVA (emulsion glaze) as a bonding medium which can be used when scenery must be washed and used again.

Scoop: Lighting instrument designed to cast unfocused light over a large area.

Score: The compilation of pages of sheet music that contains all the music for a show.

Scoring: Music added to scenes during post-production.

Scoring a Script: Breaking a monologue or scene down into beats and recording it within the text to aid in performance.

the Scottish Play: This refers to Macbeth. There is a superstition that if you utter the name of that play in a theater, bad things will happen. If you do say it, you may be asked to go outside, turn around three times and spit, and then knock to be let back into the theater. *(See Appendix: THEATER SUPERSTITIONS)*

Scout: A visit to the location to plan the work to be done there.

Scratch Track: A rough edit of the audio for a project to hear how it sounds before using it.

Screen: A flat surface on which a picture or series of pictures is projected or reflected, such as in a movie theater, or on a television set or multimedia device.

Screen Actors Guild (SAG-AFTRA): Now merged with the American Federation of Television and Radio Artists (AFTRA), SAG-AFTRA is a union that represents actors for film, television, multimedia, and commercials. *(See Appendix: ENTERTAINMENT INDUSTRY ASSOCIATIONS/ORGANIZATIONS)*

Screened, Screening: The displaying of a film or production, generally referring to a special showing as part of the production's release cycle.

Screenplay: A written piece of material by a screenwriter used for film, television, or multimedia.

Screen Test: A type of audition where an actor will be filmed performing a particular role, often not on the set or in proper wardrobe or makeup.

Screenwriter: The person responsible for writing a screenplay.

Screwball Comedy: Combines elements of farce and romantic comedy with fast-paced, witty repartee. The term is strongly associated with certain American films of the 1930-40s.

Scrim: A heatproof cloth put over lamps to diffuse the light. Or, a piece of gauze cloth that appears opaque until lit from behind, used as a screen or backdrop.

Script: A written piece of material for film, television, multimedia, or stage. The general rule of thumb is one script page equals one minute of performance time. *(See Appendixes: SPEC SCRIPT EXAMPLE and SHOOTING SCRIPT EXAMPLES)*

Script Abbreviations: In scripts, there are many abbreviations used, most of which have to do with camera shots. Here is a list of the most common script abbreviations. *(See Appendix I: SCRIPT ABBREVIATIONS)*

Script Analysis: The close study of a play or screenplay. This incorporates all of the dialogue and stage directions to find the answers necessary to create a full and rich character and to craft a performance that serves the script.

Script Girl: Takes notes during the shot about camera setup, lenses, actor dress, etc.

Scripting: The marking of a script for one character, indicating interpretation, pauses, phrasing, stress, and so on. *(Also known as Script Scoring)*

Script Reader: A person who reads screenplays for a production company.

Script Scoring: The marking of a script for one character, indicating interpretation, pauses, phrasing, stress, and so on. *(Also known as Scripting)*

Script Supervisor: The person responsible for tracking all the changes made to the script.

Scripty: Slang for the script supervisor.

Season: The annual period when the theater is most active, often from September-June, or June-August for a summer season.

Second AD: Abbreviation for Second Assistant Director.

Secondary: A medium movement.

Secondary Source: Books or other resources that help in developing characterization.

Second Assistant Cameraman: The person who takes care of film stock and uses the clapboard. *(Also known as Loader)*

Second Assistant Director: On most sets there are many 2nd AD's responsible for everything from crowd control, extras, parking, traffic control, security, cuing, script revisions, and actors on camera.

Second Cameraman: The person doing the physical filming, and often works under the cinematographer. *(Also known as Camera Operator)*

Second Meal: The meal served six hours after the end of lunch.

Second Position: Stars from an underperforming television or multimedia series start booking pilots, but the pilot role is in second position (i.e., null and void) should their current show be renewed.

Second Second AD: Abbreviation for Second Second Assistant Director.

Second Second Assistant Director: Handles paperwork for the 2nd AD. *(Also known as Third Assistant Director)*

Second Stage: A term used to describe a smaller playing area than the main stage, often for experimental or specialized theater.

Second Take: Being taped or filmed an additional time in a scene or audition allowing an actor to change his or her performance.

Second Team: A group of stand-ins and/or doubles who take the primary actors' places allowing them to rest during lighting changes and camera rehearsals.

Second Unit: A small group of filmmakers that film less important shots not involving principal actors who perform special work, such as action sequences, stunts, background shots, etc.

Segue: A transition from one shot to the other.

Selections: Wardrobe of actors or extras.

Self-Contained Artist: An artist who writes and performs his or her own material. Also refers to artists who require no production or personnel assistance from promoters.

Self-Narration: A character speaking what they think the audience needs to know about the characters or the situation.

Senior Second Assistant Director: Responsible for having extras on set at the right time, blocking extras into crowd scenes, cueing of extras, etc. *(Also known as Key Second Assistant Director)*

Sense Memory: In method acting, when an actor attempts to recall memories of the physical sensations surrounding prior emotions in order to utilize emotional memory.

Sensory: Connecting the character to the body and mind through the senses, to taste, hear, feel, see, think, perceive, and to know through the physical inner self, as opposed to the instinctive.

Separate Card: When a name appears by itself during the credits.

Sequence: The metrics used to present a time development, such as growing old. Or, a group of activities used to accomplish objectives.

Session: Meeting during which time musicians and vocalists make a recording.

Session Fee: The money the performer is paid for the day's work, usually a union scale amount.

Set: The place where filming takes place or the physical design of the stage area where the actors perform. Or, to make permanent the way a scene is being played.

Set Call Time: The moment the actor is expected to be in front of the camera or on stage in full make up and wardrobe, ready to begin working. *(Also known as Set Time)*

Set Decorator, Set Designer: The person responsible for set design.

Set Dresser: Assists the prop master and set decorator.

Set Dressing: Items placed in the scene to complement the story.

Set Piece: A piece of scenery used in a set that is not flown, but stands independent within a setting (e.g., tree, rock, etc.).

Set Props: Properties placed onstage for the use of actors.

Set Time: The expected time that the performer is required to be in front of the camera, ready and prepared. *(Also known as Set Call Time)*

Setting: Time and place of a scene.

Setup: In improv, explaining the handle or ask-for of the scene to the audience before the scene starts.

Set-Up: The time of camera changing position.

SFX: *See Sound Effects.*

Shaping: The use of beats, builds, climax, change motion, and/or resolution within a piece that give the performance things that effect rhythm, intensity, and direction. *(Also known as Orchestration)*

Share a Scene: When two actors stand or sit parallel to each other.

Sheet Music: The pages containing the music and lyrics to a single song, as opposed to a score containing all the music for a show.

Shelving: Acknowledging an offer but not doing anything with it, with the intent of using it later, however later rarely comes.

Shill: A spokesperson or promoter. Or, an accomplice of a hawker, gambler, or swindler who acts as an enthusiastic customer to entice or encourage others.

Shin Buster: The lowest lantern on a lighting boom.

Shivving: Playfully misbehaving.

Shoot: The period of actual production. Or, the act of performance.

Shoot Around You: Shooting other scenes in a script until a particular actor is available.

Shooting Schedule: A detailed list of sequence of the scenes to be shot and everything needed for each.

Shooting Script: The script as prepared for shooting, marked with directives and the scenes numbered consecutively.

Short, Short Film: A film of shorter length than a feature, usually made on a lower budget by aspiring filmmakers.

Short-Form Improv: A style of improvised theater where short and typically unrelated scenes are played, usually constructed from a predetermined game, structure, or idea and driven by an audience suggestion.

Short Reel: A short amount of footage that showcases a performer's skills. *(Also known as Demo Reel)*

Shot: An uninterrupted camera motion seen by the audience. These can be broken down into three main shot sizes: Long/Wide, Medium, and Close. Long/wide shots show the actor from a distance, emphasizing place and location, while close shots reveal details of the actor. Medium shots fall somewhere in between, putting emphasis on the character while still showing some of the surrounding environment. *(See Appendix: CAMERA SHOTS)*

Shot List: The list of shots each camera in a three camera show is to make. Or, in a single camera film, a list some directors supply for the work to be done that day, shot by shot.

Shot-Reverse-Shot: Shot of one subject, then another, then back to the first, used for conversation or reaction.

Shot Size: The relative distance of the camera which determines exactly what the edges of the frame are.

Showboat: A showoff. Or, a boat on which dramatic or musical entertainments are performed.

Showcase: An evening of scenes either prepared and rehearsed ahead of time or done as a cold reading for industry professionals to showcase new talent who may cast the actors in roles.

Show Deck: A false floor built on top of the theater stage, which contains technical elements such as automation tracks or revolves, concealed lighting or smoke effects. In some large shows, the show deck completely replaces the existing theater stage, which is put back into position when the show has finished its run.

Show Relay: A network of speakers carrying the sound of the show, and sometimes stage managers calls, to the furthest reaches of the theater.

Show Report: A written report by stage management giving problems, running times, show staff and audience numbers for the previous days' performance, circulated to the technical departments and management staff.

Showrunner: An individual ultimately responsible for the day-to-day production of a television or multimedia series.

Shtick: An entertainment routine or gimmick, helpful in securing recognition. Or, a player with a small role in a film.

Sibilance: A drawn out or excessive "S" sound during speech. In extreme cases, the "S" sound is accompanied by a whistle. Sibilance can be annoying to the audience and a hindrance to some voice actors.

Side Lighting: The type of lighting that gives the subject a mysterious feel, roughening the features.

Sides: A portion of a script selected for an audition that highlights a specific character.

Sidetracking: Changing the main story line for no reason.

Sight-and-Sound: Parent's rights under union contracts to be within the sight of the child performer at all times.

Sight Gag: A visual source of comedy, resulting from situation or props.

Sightlines: What the audience sees of the stage from where they are sitting.

Signatory: One that has signed an agreement with a union, agreeing to adhere to all the rules of that union, such as SAG-AFTRA, DGA, etc.

Signing Out: Entering the time an actor exits an audition sign-in sheet.

Sign-in Sheet: Typically used anytime there is a physical audition that will have more than five actors audition. The form serves three purposes: let the casting people know that an actor is present, organize basic contact information, and organize the order of auditions.

Signs of Character: The various cues that convey a character's personality, emotion or motivation.

Signs of Performance: An actor's movements, expressions and vocal tones and patterns that contribute to signs of character.

Silent Bit: When an actor or extra performs a noticeable or required action in a scene, but with no lines.

Silent on Camera (SOC): A shot taken without any sound or dialogue, many times referred to as "mit out sound," attributed to one theory that a 1920s director with a heavy German accent pronounced it that way. *(Also known as Mit Out Sound or Motion Only Shot or Motor Only Shot or Motor Only Sync)*

Simplify: Strip away extemporaneous movements both physically and psychologically in order get to the core of communication or action.

Simultaneous Dialogue: When two characters speak at the same time, written in the script in two columns side by side.

Singing Voice: The person who performs an actor's vocal parts in the dubbing process in post-production.

Single. Recording released by a record company.

Sister Union: One or more additional unions an actor joins after the first one. The first union joined is the parent union.

Sitcom: Abbreviation for Situation Comedy, a half hour situational comedy show on television or multimedia.

Site Specific: A play which is created or specifically modified to use the character of the performance space to the greatest advantage. Site specific spaces are usually locations which are not normally used for showcasing theater, but have another primary function, such as a warehouse, mansion, sports stadium, etc.

Situational Irony: What is expected and actually happens due to forces beyond human control.

Situation Comedy: A humorous television or multimedia show where the storyline focuses on a relatively stable set of characters, such as members of a family or a group of coworkers.

Sitzprobe: Meaning seated rehearsal, it is the first rehearsal of the singers with the orchestra and no acting.

Six Elements of Tragedy: Plot, character, diction, thought, spectacle (scenic effect), and song (music), of which the first two are primary. *(Also known as Aristotle's Six Elements of Drama)*

Size Card: A form filled out at casting sessions or on set to inform wardrobe people of an actor's clothing size.

Sketch: A short, funny play or filmed performance usually consisting of one scene.

Skin Money: Extra payment made to actors when nudity is required on set.

Skins: List of people working who have been booked for that particular day.

Skip: A large wicker basket or box, often wheeled, which stores costumes and/or props for touring.

Skull Cap: Plastic head-shaped covering to give appearance of baldness.

Skycloth: Another term for cyclorama, a curved plain cloth or plastered wall filling the rear of the stage or studio.

SL: Abbreviation for Stage Left. *(See Appendix: STAGE DIRECTION ABBREVIATIONS)*

Slapstick: Relies on highly physical and visual humor, often featuring violent and aggressive action, but usually without serious harm or pain to the characters.

Slate: A quick statement to the camera of a performer's name and agency, and any additional required details before the audition begins. Or, an audible announcement of the take number recorded ahead of a take. Or, the slate board itself. *(Also known as Slating)*

Slate Board: A chalkboard with a clapper on top used as a visual cue for the camera and to mark the shot being filmed. *(Also known as Clapboard or Clapper or Clapperboard)*

Slating: A quick statement to the camera of a performer's name and agency, and any additional required details before the audition begins. Or, an audible announcement of the take number recorded ahead of a take. Or, the slate board itself. *(Also known as Slate)*

Sleeper: A show that is an unexpected success.

Slice-of-Life Commercial: A miniature play that quickly identifies a problem and just as quickly offers a solution.

Slightly Restricted: A term used when applications for a dramatic work are being accepted on a case-by-case basis because of current or future major city tours.

Slow Motion: When time moves slowly in film.

Slow Stock: A type of film which creates a more even and polished image, at the expense of requiring well lit and consistent conditions.

Slugline: A short description of the location and time of day of a scene (e.g., EXT. CABIN - DAY). *(Also known as Scene Heading)*

Small: A very subtle performance by an actor.

Smash Cut: A quick or sudden cut from one scene to another.

Smoke Machine: Electrically powered unit which produces clouds of white non-toxic fog (available in different flavors/smells) by the vaporization of mineral oil. Specially designed for theater & film use. Vital for revealing airborne light beams. *(Also known as Fog Machine)*

Snap Line: Chalked piece of string which, when stretched tight and snapped is used for marking straight lines on stage or on scenery as a painting aid.

Snap To: Blackout is achieved instantly.

Soap, Soap Opera: A serial drama on television or multimedia that examines the lives of many characters, usually focusing on emotional relationships to the point of melodrama. Originally, these were only radio or daytime television dramas sponsored by the makers of laundry detergent.

SOC: *See Silent on Camera.*

Social Actor: People who portray themselves in a performance, usually previously known to the audience.

Soft Focus: A degree of focus where things are slightly blurred, often used for romanticism.

Sold Out: When the number of tickets sold for a performance is equal to or greater than the number of available seats.

Soliloquy: Monologue that usually represents the inner workings of one character's perspective, given directly to the audience, sometimes played as a character thinking aloud in the audience's presence.

Soubrette: A female performer playing a lively, flirtatious role in a play or opera. Or, a minor female role, such as a maid, in comedy.

Sound and Light Lock: A vestibule that separates the auditorium from the lobby, or the stage from the back of house, to keep noise and light out of the auditorium.

Sound Check: A thorough test of the sound system before a performance.

Sound Cue: Sound effects, such as music, a doorbell, a car door, a dog barking, etc.

Sound Designer: Responsible for designing sound directions during a staged show.

Sound Editor: Coordinates music and effect tracks.

Sound Effects (FX, SFX): Noises used to accompany a scene on stage.

Sound FX: Abbreviation for Sound Effects.

Sound Mixer: Responsible for all sound recording on the set during the production. There are also sound mixers who do re-recording of the show with sound effects and music in the final mix. *(Also known as Location Sound Engineer or Production Sound Mixer)*

Sound Operator: The person who puts the microphones on the actors, and records the sound.

Sound Reinforcement: Amplifying a voice just enough so that it can be heard, without the audience being aware that it is being amplified.

Sound Stage: A special building designed for film production.

Space Object: An object that's used in the scene that doesn't really exist. A mimed object.

Speaker: Device used to amplify sound. Or, the person talking.

Spear Carriers: A slang term for extras.

Spec: The people who arrive on the set when they're not booked.

Spec: A script written without being commissioned on the speculative hope that it is sold. It is written without camera directions or scene numbers. *(Also known as Spec Script)*

Special: Usually a spotlight not used for general illumination, but for a special effect, such a lighting a single actor in one place. Or, it can be a guest role, a funny one-liner, or a very featured background role.

Special Effects (SPFX): Illusions or visual tricks to simulate the imagined events in a story.

Specifically Upstaging: Pulling focus on purpose by moving upstage to make another actor's back face the audience.

Spec Script: A script written without being commissioned on the speculative hope that it is sold. It is written without camera directions or scene numbers. *(Also known as Spec)*

Spectacle: Scenery, music and costumes. Or, a public show or display, especially on a large scale.

Speculative: Creating something, such as a script, with no buyer yet.

Speed: A command from a crew member that indicates the film and the audiotape are running simultaneously at the correct speed and are ready for filming.

Speed-Through: A rehearsal with actors going through the lines of the play as quickly as possible, picking up the cues.

SPFX: *See Special Effects.*

Spider: Adapter to connect many lighting instruments to one multicore cable.

Spike: Marking the stage to indicate where the props and furniture will be placed.

Spiking the Lens: An actor looking directly into the camera during a take.

Spill: Unwanted light onstage.

Spinto: A lyric voice that has the power and incisiveness for dramatic climaxes.

Spirit Gum: A quick-drying solution of gum, mainly used by actors to attach false hair to their faces.

Split Publishing: When the publishing rights to a song are divided among two or more publishers.

Split Screen: Separates the screen into fragments, each containing its own shot.

Spokesperson Commercial: Uses an authority figure or celebrity to lend credibility to a product.

Spontaneity: A free unplanned impulsive moment.

Spontaneous Improvisation: Performance created on the spot without a script or plan.

Spoof: A production that pokes fun at certain subjects or time periods.

Spot: A commercial.

Spotlight: A type of light whose beam is focused through a lens or series of lenses to make it more controllable. Or, to highlight someone or put them in the limelight.

Spotting: Locating where the sound effects and music will go in the locked cut.

Spreading the Shot: One actor stands too far from the other which spreads the shot out.

SQ: Abbreviation for Sound Cue.

Squeezebox: On television or multimedia, the picture box inserted to show another picture without cutting away.

Squib: A small radio controlled explosive device on an actor's body that simulates a bullet-shot on the body and similar effects such as fake blood.

SR: Abbreviation for Stage Right. *(See Appendix: STAGE DIRECTION ABBREVIATIONS)*

SRO: *See Standing Room Only.*

Stable: The roster of performers an agent represents.

Stage: The area where actors perform.

Stage Areas: The various sections of the stage. Left and right are as seen by those on stage, not in the audience. Since many stages are raked, meaning higher in back than in front, upstage is at the back and downstage at the front.

Stage Business: A smaller stage activity used to accent, intensify, or heighten the manner where one uses an object on stage, such as painting a picture, or pouring coffee, etc.

Stage Combat: A specialized technique in designed to create the illusion of physical combat without causing harm to the performers by using fight choreography.

Stage Convention: Any action that would be odd in real life, but accepted as normal on stage, such as a stage whisper, ensemble singing, soliloquies, etc.

Stagecraft: Skill in, or the art of, producing or participating in the production of a dramatic piece, especially in the technical area.

Stage Crew: The backstage technical crew responsible for running the show.

Stage Directions: The director's insertions of blocking, reactions, gestures, or use of props to clarify the action.

Stage Director: The one responsible for deciding the interpretation of each character, the movements of the singers on stage, and other things affecting the singers and is in charge at rehearsals.

Stage Door: A back entrance to the theater used by the cast and production crew.

Stage Electrician: Member of the electrics staff whose responsibility it is to set or clear electrics equipment during scene changes.

Stage Fright: Anxiety during the performance.

Stagehand: One who works behind-the-scenes setting up lighting, props, rigging, scenery and special effects for a production.

Stage House: The part of a theater building upstage of the proscenium wall that includes the stage, wings, galleries, gridirons, etc.

Stage Left: In a proscenium theater, the actor's left, while facing the audience.

Stage Manager: The person responsible for running the whole show and the director's liaison backstage during rehearsal and performance.

Stage Presence: Strength of character and performance that draws the audience to a performer.

Stage Right: In a proscenium theater, the actor's left, while facing the audience.

Stage Weight: Cast iron weight placed to prevent movement of props. *(Also known as Brace Weight or Pig Iron)*

Stage Whisper: Sounds like a whisper but is loud enough for the audience to hear.

Stagger-Through: The first tentative attempt to run through the whole show.

Staging: The final results of blocking.

Stakes: The heightened consequences for each character of achieving or failing to achieve their objectives.

Stalls: The lowest seating section of the theater and normally closest to the stage.

Stand and Deliver: To direct a monologue to the audience but still engage the other actors in the scene.

Standard: A song or movie that continues to be popular for several years.

Standby: The command for actors to be ready for their cue for action.

Standby: An actor or performer who will appear in a particular role if the regular performer is not present. *(Also known as Understudy)*

Standby Cue: Notification of an upcoming action or cue, indicated in the prompt book. *(Also known as Warn Cue)*

Stand-In: Performer used for size and coloring to double for a principal actor for lighting and camera set ups.

Standing Ovation: At the end of a performance, when the audience stands and claps, a higher form of praise than normal applause.

Standing Room: A space where people can stand to watch a performance, especially if all the seats are filled.

Standing Room Only (SRO): Admittance to a performance after all of the seats are filled which requires people to stand to watch.

Stanislavski, Konstantin: (1863-1938) Russian theater director, actor, and teacher most responsible for the manner and technique where the craft of acting is taught. He developed a method where actors could consistently produce superior work by tapping into themselves and their real feelings, to create naturalistic acting as opposed to the representational acting style popular at the time.

Star: An actor in a lead role. Or, an actor who has gained celebrity status.

Starlet: A young female actress who is gaining in popularity.

State-of-the-Art: Contemporary or current.

Station 12: Report which a casting director must obtain from SAG-AFTRA before employing one of its actors.

Status: A level of power given to a character through three tools: simplicity, focus, and control. A character's sense of self-worth. Many scenes are built around status transfers, in which one character's status drops while another's rises. Physical environments and objects also have status.

Status Quo: The existing state of affairs of the main character's daily life and their world.

Statutory Copyright: Status acquired by a composition when it is registered with the Copyright Office or is published with the proper copyright notice.

Steadicam: This mechanism stabilizes hand-held camera shot and uses a gyroscope.

Steal, Steal Focus, Stealing a Scene: Attracting attention from the person to whom the audience's interest legitimately belongs.

Stealing Shots: Quickly and secretly getting shots at a location without film permits, usually with a skeleton crew.

Step Into It: For an actor to stay one step out of frame, and then to step in.

Stepping on Lines: A term used for when one actor cuts off another actor, not to be confused with interruption.

Stepping Out: Breaking the reality of the scene. *(Also known as Commenting)*

Stereotypical Characters: An oversimplified image or idea of a particular type of person or thing.

Sticks: Slang for the clapboard/slateboard which is the chalkboard with a clapper on top used as a visual cue for the camera that marks the shot being filmed. Or, slang for a tripod.

Still: A photograph that is not a series of frames.

Stock Character: A stereotyped character, continually to used in one form or another, such as the servant, the miser, the clown, etc.

Stock Company: An acting company whose members play all the roles in a series of plays, as opposed to casting each play separately.

Stock Footage: Footage of events in history from other films, television, or multimedia broadcasts.

Stock Rights: Royalty paid for a play used by a stock company.

Stock Shot: A shot made of pre-existing footage. *(Also known as Library Shot)*

Stooge: An entertainer who feeds lines to the main comedian and usually serves as the butt of their jokes. Or, any underling, assistant, or accomplice.

Storage Plot: A diagram showing how scenic units are to be stored in the wing areas during a show.

Story: The plot of a novel, play, movie, or other narrative form. *(Also known as Storyline)*

Storyboard: A frame-by-frame artist's drawing of key scenes with the dialogue printed underneath serving as a rough plan for the way the commercial or film should appear and what camera angles the director should use.

Storyline: The plot of a novel, play, movie, or other narrative form. *(Also known as Story)*

Straight Part: A role where the actor and the character portrayed are similar in appearance and personality.

Straight Person: An entertainer who feeds lines to the main comedian and usually serves as the butt of their jokes.

Strasberg, Lee: (1901-1982) Acting teacher, artistic director of the Actor's Studio, and developer of what came to be known as method acting. Strasberg intensely focused on actors exploring past memories to use real emotions to connect them to their character.

Strategy: How a character goes about achieving their goal. *(Also known as Tactics)*

Strike, Strike Structure: To remove something from or take apart the stage set.

Strip Programming: A system of showing a program in the same time period five times a week.

Studio: A room or a building where the filming on the set takes place. Or, a company that oversees the approval of concepts leading to the creation and production of major motion pictures. Or, an audio isolation room where the talent performs, with an adjoining control room.

Studio Hire: Union term for actors who work in the same area where they are hired or reside.

Studio Lot: Administrative offices and production facilities for a studio, with tightly controlled access through a limited number of gates.

Studio Teacher: Set teacher or tutor, hired to provide education to working with young performers, and is also responsible for enforcing child labor laws.

Studio Work: Filming done on the studio lot.

Studio Zone: The radius centered at the intersection of West Beverly Blvd and North La Cienega Blvd in Los Angeles, significant because it was the former home of AMPAS, who created the zone to establish a reasonable distance that union workers should be expected to travel to and from the production location without additional compensation. *(Also known as Thirty-Mile Zone)*

Stunt: A scene in a production that requires physical actions that are considered dangerous. Or, a publicity event designed to call attention to a project or a particular actor.

Stunt Coordinator: The person who's responsible for coordinating all the stunts performed by actors or stand-ins.

Stunt Double: The person who performs all the stunts instead of the principal actor.

Stunt Pay: Additional hazard money paid to an actor or stunt double to perform dangerous scenes.

Stunt Person: A person who performs stunts during filming.

Style: The distinctive and unique manner of a writer, director, or performer.

Subject: What a story or play is about, to be distinguished from plot and theme.

Subjective Acting: Actors play their parts in such a way that they actually weep, suffer, or struggle emotionally as they become their character. *(Also known as Emotional Acting)*

Subjective Camera: Shots simulating what a character actually sees, meaning the audience, the character, and camera all see the same thing.

Subjective Shot: The audience (camera) will see what the character sees.

Submission: Suggestion of actors for roles.

Subplot: A secondary, subordinate, or auxiliary plot line, often complementary but independent from the main plot, and often involving supporting characters.

Subplot Characters: These characters either help, initiate, complicate, or fight the protagonist's efforts.

Substitution: The use of an actor's personal experience to relate to the experience of a character in a play.

Subtext: The character's complex thoughts, feelings, motives, etc., created and layered under the actual words and actions of the character by the actor.

Subtitles: Text translations at the bottom of the screen of the words being spoken on by the performers.

Suggested Setting: A setting where a few set pieces take the place of elaborate set construction.

Summer Stock: Repertory theater that produces shows during summer time.

Sun Getting Yellow: At the end of the day, it means that the sun is going down and the light is getting weak.

Super: Slang term for extras. *(Also known as Supernumeraries)*

SUPER: Abbreviation for SUPERIMPOSE.

SUPERIMPOSE: The laying of one image on top of another, usually words over a filmed scene, always typed in CAPS.

Superimposition: Two distinct images appearing simultaneously with one superimposed upon the other. *(Also known as Double Exposure)*

Supernumeraries: Another term for extras. *(Also known as Super)*

Super Objective: Konstantin Stanislavski developed the concept of the character's long term objective or big dream in life. It does not necessarily apply directly to any single scene, but has an effect on every scene. *(Also known as Happiness)*

Superstar: Someone who is extremely famous. *(Also known as Megastar)*

Superstition: A belief or practice resulting from ignorance, fear of the unknown, trust in magic or chance, or a false conception of causation, very popular in theater. *(See Appendix: THEATER SUPERSTITIONS)*

Supertitles: Translations of the words being sung, or the actual words if the libretto is in the native language, that are projected on a screen above the stage.

Supervising Sound Editor: Oversees the sound mixing process.

Supporting Cast: Actors who are not playing major parts.

Supporting Role: A smaller role than lead, but larger than extra, with some acting and speaking parts.

SW: Abbreviation for Start Work, the term used on the call sheet to indicate an actor commencing work on that particular day.

Swag: A particularly artistic way of drawing a set of tabs/drapes diagonally up at the same time as flying them out. Or, a goodie bag that contains various items, usually given at parties by sponsors or to the cast at the end of the run of the show.

Sweeps Months: Local television stations use the ratings during the months of February, May, July, and November to set their basic advertising rates for the next three-month period.

Sweeten: The addition of new parts to existing rhythms and vocal tracks.

SWF: Abbreviation for Start Work Finish, a notation on a call sheet that indicates when an actor is starting, working, and finished on that day.

Swing: A member of the cast who understudies multiple roles in the production.

Swish Pan: A pan shot with extreme blur.

SX: Abbreviation for Sound.

Symbolic Characters: One-dimensional, usually personifying only one quality or idea, such as love, wisdom, or mercy.

Synchronization: The placing of music to film with exact timing.

Synchronization Right: The right to use a musical composition in a film or video.

Synchronous Sound: Sound which is in sync with the image on screen.

Syndication: A show is sold to be broadcast in local or regional markets.

Synopsis: A summary written description of a script's plot.

Syntax: The grammatical order of words in a sentence or line of verse or dialogue.

Synthesis: In improv, combining two dissimilar ideas into one, such as hearing two suggestions from the audience and combining them into a single idea that gets used in the scene.

T

Tab: Any stage curtains including a vertically flying front curtain (house tabs) and especially a pair of horizontally moving curtains which overlap at the center and move outwards from that center. Or, short for tabloid, referring to a condensed version of a show.

Tab Dressing: Lighting focused onto the house tabs.

Tableau: A silent and motionless depiction of a scene created by actors, often from a picture.

Table Read: When an organized reading of the script around a table by the actors with speaking parts is conducted.

Tabs: The curtains separating the stage from the audience.

Tactics: How a character goes about achieving their goal. *(Also known as Strategy)*

Taft-Hartley Law: Law that allows non-union actors to work under a union contract for their first role. After that, they must join the union.

Tag: A short scene at the end of a production that usually provides some upbeat addition to the climax. Commercial tags are often delivered by a voice talent different from those in the main body of the ad.

Tagline: A catchphrase or slogan, especially as used in advertising, or the punchline of a joke, usually humorous or clever.

Tag Out: In improv, tapping a player on the shoulder, and replacing that player, then the scene moves on.

Tails Out: Recording tape wound on a reel so that the end of the soundtrack is on the outside. A tape wound tails out is usually marked with blue adhesive tape, while one wound heads out is usually marked with red adhesive tape.

Take: The shooting of a scene.

Take 5: Abbreviation for Take Five.

Take Camera: Direction to the actor to turn toward the camera so that the audience will get the full effect of his reaction to dialog or action.

Take Five: A five minute break during rehearsal.

Taking the Stage: Giving an actor the freedom to move over the entire stage area, usually during a lengthy speech.

Taking Yourself Out of a Scene: The actor's turning away from the audience into a three-quarter-back or full-back position.

Talent: All above-the-line personnel, but specifically the actors.

Talent #1, 2, 3, etc.: Unless the character in a script is given a name or description (e.g., Old Man, Nurse, etc.), they are noted as Talent #1, 2, etc.

Talent Agent: Agency or person that represents performers and suggests them to casting directors for auditions, negotiates contracts, takes care of schedules, payments and anything involving their client.

Talent Release: A document the talent signs that gives the filmmaker permission to distribute and sell the film. *(Also known as General Release)*

Talent Scout: Hired by studios and casting agencies to search for fresh star talent.

Talkback: The system that allows people in the control room to talk with the talent in the studio.

Talking Heads: An actor or host on a television or multimedia program who speaks directly to the audience and who is usually shown only from the shoulders up. Or. a scene that involves a lot of standing or sitting around talking rather than engaging in physical action.

Tape: A video tape compilation of an actor's best work. *(Also known as Reel)*

Taping: The final performance of a sitcom episode, usually with a live audience.

Tasks: Pieces of work or functions that need to be done, the total of which comprises an overall activity.

TBC: Abbreviation for To Be Confirmed, or To Be Cast.

Tear Sheets: Copy of a print ad or article from a newspaper or magazine.

Teaser: The short scene on a television or multimedia show that comes before the opening credits. *(Also known as Cold or Cold Opening)*

Teasers: The wide horizontal curtains or flats over the acting area that conceal the lights and other technical things overhead. *(Also known as Borders)*

Tech: Abbreviation for Technical Rehearsal.

Techie: A slang term for a member of the technical crew of a show.

Technical Acting: Use of learned skills of acting, movement, speech, and interpretation to create roles where no emotional response is used and performance based on technique. *(Also known as Objective Acting)*

Technical Cue: Any technical change or event.

Technical Demands: The extent to which a play requires specific lighting, sound, sets, etc.

Technical Director: The person responsible for supervising construction of a stage set.

Technical Rehearsal: The first time the play is rehearsed at the location it's going to be seen later by an audience.

Technicolor: A process of color cinematography using synchronized monochrome films, each of a different color, to produce a movie, television, or multimedia show in color.

Technique Actor: Actor who imitates a certain behavior on camera.

Telegraphing: Broad charade-type actions used by inexperienced actors to get a point across. Or, when the author reveals what is going to happen before it actually happens, which kills the suspense.

Telephoto: An extremely long-ranged lens.

Teleplay: A script written or adapted for television or multimedia.

Teleprompter: A device that allows for the reader to look right into the camera while reading the scripted dialogue on a screen, usually placed directly under the camera.

Telescoping: When a character reacts to a stimuli before it actually takes place.

Television (TV): A mass telecommunication medium used for transmitting moving images for entertainment, education, news, politics, gossip, and advertising. Or, the actual device on which a program is viewed.

Tempo: The level of speed with which the scene or play is acted out. The general effect creates a specific mood or tone to the work.

Ten-Minute Play: A complete play, with a beginning, middle and end, designed to play in ten minutes.

Tennis-Court Staging: The staging of a performance with the audience placed on two sides, as though the performance space is a street. *(Also known as Alley Staging or Avenue Staging)*

Tension: The atmosphere created by unresolved, disquieting, or inharmonious situations that human beings feel compelled to address.

Tertiary: A small movement.

Test Audience: Special screenings used to gauge the reaction of the group, and help determine certain scenes to be dropped and new ones added.

Test Commercial: A commercial that will be aired in a small area and monitored for its effectiveness.

Text: Printed words, including dialogue and the stage directions for a script.

That's a Wrap: Command that filming has ended for the day or for the whole production.

Theater: Building where acting takes place. Or, the world of acting in general as in the art itself. *(Also known as Theatre)*

Theater Arts: The collective name for lighting, sound, costume, props, makeup and set.

Theater in the Round: Any theater where the audience is seated on every side of the stage.

Theater of Alienation: An acting style or form of theater based on the principle of using live performance as a means of social and political commentary. This started as a theatrical movement of the early 1920-30s, characterized by the use of such artificial devices as cartoons, posters, and film sequences distancing the audience from theatrical illusion and following focus on the play's message. *(See Dialetical Theater or Epic Theater)*

Theater of the Absurd: Theatrical movement beginning in the 1950s where playwrights created works representing the universe as unknowable and humankind's existence as meaningless.

Theater Literacy: The ability to create, perform, perceive, analyze, critique, and understand dramatic performances.

Theater Superstitions: Theater is filled with superstitions and traditions that have been passed down from generation to generation. *(See Appendix: THEATER SUPERSTITIONS)*

Theatre: Building where acting takes place. Or, the world of acting in general as in the art itself. *(Also known as Theater)*

Theatrical: Of or relating to the stage.

Theatrical Conventions: The established techniques, practices, and devices unique to theatrical productions.

Theatrical Experiences: Events, activities, and productions associated with theater, film, video, and multimedia.

Theatrical Film: A series of still images which, when shown on a screen, creates the illusion of moving images. Or, to capture on film as part of a series of moving images as in make a movie of a story or event. *(Also known as Film or Motion Picture or Movie or Photoplay)*

The Business: Show business in general.

The Ear: Information is transmitted to an earpiece through a loop around the neck. *(Also known as Ear Prompter)*

Theme: The idea of a literary work abstracted from its details of language, character, and action, and cast in the form of a generalization.

Thesp, Thespian: An actor. Or, relating to drama and the theater.

Thespis: (550-500 BC) A Greek poet, usually considered the founder of drama because he was the first one to use an actor in addition to the chorus in his plays. Some theater historians believe that Thespis was that first actor. Although none of his plays remain, some titles are known: Phorbus, The Priests, The Youths, and Pentheus.

Third AD: Abbreviation for Third Assistant Director.

Third Assistant Director: Handles anything assigned by the 2nd AD. *(Also known as Second Second Assistant Director)*

Thirty-Mile Zone (TMZ): The radius centered at the intersection of West Beverly Boulevard and North La Cienega Boulevard in Los Angeles, California, significant because it was the former home of the Academy of Motion Picture Arts and Sciences, who created the zone to establish a reasonable distance that union workers should be expected to travel to and from the production location without additional compensation. *(Also known as Studio Zone)*

Thought Tracking: When a character speaks out loud about their inner thoughts.

Thought Tunnel: When characters walk past other characters who comment on their situation.

Three Bells: An indication to be quiet on the set during the filming of the scene.

Three-Camera: When three cameras are used to film a television or multimedia show, used widely for sitcoms and news shows. Generally, the two outer cameras shoot close-up shots or crosses of the two most active characters on the set at any given time, while the central camera or cameras shoot a wider master shot to capture the overall action and establish the geography of the room. In this way, multiple shots are obtained in a single take without having to start and stop the action.

Three Major Meanings: The passions of a character that have the greatest significance in their life. The meanings are what give a character three dimensions and make up the core purpose of a character. *(Also known as Major Meanings)*

Three-Quarters: A stage position in a proscenium theater, where the actor is facing half-way toward the actor to their side and half-way toward the audience. Thus the audience is essentially seeing a three-quarter view of the actor.

Three Quarter Shot: A variation between the medium and full shot, this one frames a person from the knees up.

Three Shot (Two, Three, Four, etc.): Designates the number of actors in the frame.

Throughline: The combined series of actions that are mapped out in a script by an actor in working out their character's story moment by moment, scene by scene.

Through Line of Action: Konstantin Stanislavski's concept of the inner line of effort that guides the actors from the beginning to the end of the play.

Throw: Distance between a light source and the actor or object being lit.

Throw Away: To underemphasize or underplay liens or stage business, either deliberately or aimlessly.

Thrust, Thrust Stage: A stage that extends out into the audience, so that the audience is seated on three sides of it.

Thunder Sheet: Large suspended steel sheet with handles which produces a thunder-like rumble when shaken or beaten.

Tight Cowboy: Getting its name from the westerns of the 1930-40s, this camera shot frames the actor from above the guns on their hip.

Tight-On, Tight Shot: A shot that focuses on a single subject and allows for very little to no extra space around.

Tilt Shot: The camera is set at an angle so the horizon line is not level, often used to show a disoriented psychological state. *(Also known as Dutch Angle Shot)*

Tilts: A way to advance a scene, or to cause status change. A classic tilt would be a couple at the breakfast table, where the woman announces out of the blue that she's pregnant.

Timbre: The color/tone of sound. Or, the roughness of a voice.

TIME CUT: Used as a transition in a script, when the intent is to cut to later in a scene.

Time Dash: In the course of a scene (or a whole performance), show the characters at a different point in (story) time than the one in which they were introduced.

Time In, Time Out: The headings on an audition sign-in sheet where you indicate the time you arrived and the time you left.

Time Sheet: Lists the names of all the performers who worked that day, including the time they were there and is used to calculate the payment to the performer. *(Also known as Performers Work Report)*

Timing: Best moment for an actor to do something or say something.

Title Page: A page of the script that contains the title and author's name for a spec script, and additional names on the shooting script.

Title Sequence: The method by which films, television, or multimedia shows present their title, key production and cast members, using conceptual visuals and sound.

TMZ: *See Thirty-Mile Zone.* Also the name of a celebrity gossip series produced by Harvey Levin Productions.

Tone: The general character or attitude of a place, piece of writing, situation, etc. Or, a musical or vocal sound with reference to its pitch, quality, and strength.

To Ones: Slang term meaning the actors and set should be returned to their positions and the way it was at the beginning of the scene. *(Also known as Back-to-One or From the Top or Reset)*

Tooth Varnish: Used to create the look of missing tooth by blacking out an existing one.

Top: To make a line stronger than the line or lines preceding it by speaking at a higher pitch, at a faster rate, or with greater volume and emphasis.

Top Billing: The first name on the advertisement or in the credits for a production.

Top Hat: Cylinder of metal inserted into color runners on the front of a lantern to limit spill light.

Topical Reference: A brand name or a dated trendy detail that may not be understood by all audiences later.

Top Lighting: The type of lighting that spiritualizes the subject.

Top of Show: In theater, this refers to the condition of the stage at the moment the curtain rises and/or the lights go up at the beginning of the play (i.e., specifically, the position of props and set pieces). Or, in television or multimedia, this refers to the highest rate a day player can receive for an appearance on the series.

Topping a Line: An actor responding with a line that is more powerful than the one delivered before them.

Top Shot: Taken from directly overhead and from a distance, often from on a crane or helicopter. *(Also known as Bird's Eye View Shot)*

Tormentors, Torms: Masking curtains hung vertically on the sides of the performing area and hide offstage areas from the view of the audience. *(Also known as Legs)*

Touring Company: A company of performers who travel with a show that they present in essentially the same way it was, originally created in a theater center such as New York City.

Track: One of the several components of special recording tape that contains recorded sounds, instruments or voices of a particular music section that are recorded separately.

Tracking Shot: A shot where the camera is moved on a track or by means of wheels, such as a dolly, a car, a train, etc. *(Also known as Traveling Shot)*

Trades: Industry newspapers, magazines, and other media read by all industry professionals to keep up with trends and news in the entertainment business.

Tragedy: A play that is serious and ends unhappily. The protagonist in a tragedy frequently faces an ethical choice or a choice about a moral issue. Or, the stage area away from the audience. Or, to steal the focus of a scene.

Tragic Flaw: A weakness or limitation of character, resulting in the fall of the tragic hero.

Tragic Force: Action working against the hero.

Tragic Hero: A privileged, exalted character of high repute, who, by virtue of a tragic flaw and fate, suffers a fall from glory into suffering.

Tragicomedy: When tragic and comic qualities are equally mixed.

Trailer: A mobile dressing room for an actor.

Trailer: The preview advertisement for a film. *(Also known as Preview)*

Transaction Scene: A scene where nothing happens but a simple transaction.

Transference: Uta Hagen's term for the actor's process of making transferences from their own experiences to those in the play until they become synonymous with them.

Transformation: An instant scene change, often effected by exploiting the varying transparency of gauze under different lighting conditions.

Transition: A script notation denoting a transition within the telling of a story. For example, DISSOLVE TO: means the action blurs and refocuses into another scene, and is generally used to denote a passage of time.

Transitions: Mechanisms, mainly used to end a scene and move on to the next scene.

Transverse: Form of staging where the audience is on either side of the acting area.

Trap, Trap Door: An opening on the stage where something or someone can be hidden.

Trap Room: The area directly below the trapped part of the stage, used for accessing the traps.

Traveler, Traveler Curtain: The most common type of front curtain used in theaters that remain at a fixed elevation and open and close horizontally, breaking in the middle.

Traveling Shot: A shot where the camera is moved on a track or by means of wheels, such as a dolly, a car, a train, etc. *(Also known as Tracking Shot)*

Treading the Boards: Walking on the stage.

Treads: General name for any stage staircase or set of steps.

Treatment: More detailed explanation of the story or plot. A shortened version to a full script which includes a short description of the story and the characters involved, and typically ranges from one to ten pages in length. *(Also known as Outline)*

Trigger: An emotional or physical signal that signals for emotion to break through to the surface.

Trim: A pre-plotted height for a piece of scenery or lighting bar, usually measured against the height of the teaser.

Triple Threat: Refers to an actor or actress who can sing, dance and act skillfully and equally well on a consistent basis, usually applicable to performers in the musicals genre, but it also refers to a person who can act, direct, and write.

Troop: A theater company formed by a group of actors. *(Also known as Troupe)*

Trooper: A performer/crew that works despite adversity. Or, a team player. *(Also known as Trouper)*

Troupe: A theater company formed by a group of actors. *(Also known as Troop)*

Trouper: A performer/crew that works despite adversity. Or, a team player. *(Also known as Trooper)*

Trouser Role: A role depicting a young man or boy but performed by a woman. *(Also known as Pants Role)*

Truck: A platform on wheels, where scenery can be mounted and rolled into any position on stage.

Trucking Shot: Any shot made from a vehicle.

Tumbling: Flying a drop from the bottom as well as the top when there is insufficient height to fly it in the normal way.

Tummeling: Bantering with the audience during setups.

Turkey: A performance that fails miserably.

Turn: Slang crew term for actor or artist. (e.g., When is the turn call?)

Turnaround: Shot from a different direction. Or, the cast and crew rest time, from wrap until next day's call time. Or, a project, which was previously picked up by a production entity, but has been dropped and is currently in a state of limbo allowing the producers to set up the project with another studio.

Turning the Scene In: Focusing audience attention on the actor who is the real center of the dramatic action by having the other actors shift their bodies and look at this key character.

Turn Over: What the director says to signal the cameraman to begin filming. *(Also known as Roll Camera)*

TV: Abbreviation for Television.

Twist: A surprising, yet explainable and motivated change in the direction of the action, either within a scene, a sequence, or in the overall story line.

Two Shot (Two, Three, Four, etc.): Designates the number of actors in the frame.

Two Shot West: A shot where one character will turn 180° and face away from the other character while they continue to talk, which enables both characters to appear together in a single shot facing the audience, used commonly in soap operas.

Two-Walling: When the entertainer is responsible for some of the costs related to the show and the venue owner pays the rest. The owner then divides the profits with the entertainer in an agreed-upon split. *(Also known as Pay-to-Play)*

Type: What the actor would be typecast as, such as girl next door, nerd, tough guy, rebel, funny one, best friend, etc.

Typecast: When an actor becomes associated with only one type of role or character, often based on physical appearance.

Typecasting: Assigning a role to an actor on the basis of his or her surface appearance or personality.

Typed-out: The elimination of an actor during auditions because of such obvious features as height, weight or age.

U

U: Abbreviation for Upstage. *(See Appendix: STAGE DIRECTION ABBREVIATIONS)*

U5: Abbreviation for Under-Five.

Uber-Mime: Overly elaborate mime that is so detailed it is hard to follow.

UC: Abbreviation for Upstage Center. *(See Appendix: STAGE DIRECTION ABBREVIATIONS)*

UL: Abbreviation for Upstage Left. *(See Appendix: STAGE DIRECTION ABBREVIATIONS)*

ULC: Abbreviation for Upstage Left Center. *(See Appendix: STAGE DIRECTION ABBREVIATIONS)*

ULCS: Abbreviation for Upstage Left Center. *(See Appendix: STAGE DIRECTION ABBREVIATIONS)*

ULS: Abbreviation for Upstage Left. *(See Appendix: STAGE DIRECTION ABBREVIATIONS)*

Uncle Buddy: Slang for a bar that works by friction against the ropes to let a piece in or out under control. *(Also known as Buddy Bar)*

Underacting: An actor whose performance is not big or over the top at all, often used in a complimentary sense.

Under-Five (U5): An acting role designation calling for five lines or less. This category has a specific pay rate, which is less than a day player.

Underscore: Term for the music that accompanies a film.

Understudy: An actor who learns a role to substitute in case principal actors cannot perform. *(Also known as Standby)*

Union: Unions are responsible for protecting performers' rights, as well as regulating pay and working hours, such as AEA, SAG-AFTRA, etc.

Union Scale: Minimum wage scale earned in employment by members of AF of M, SAG-AFTRA, etc.

United States Institute for Theater Technology (USITT): A nonprofit serving the performing arts design, theater tech and production fields. *(See Appendix: ENTERTAINMENT INDUSTRY ASSOCIATIONS/ORGANIZATIONS)*

Unities: The idea that a play should be limited to a specific time, place, and story line, or more specifically, the events of the plot should occur within a twenty-four hour period, within a given geographic locale, and should tell a single story.

Unit Move: Same day of shooting, with a physical location move.

Unit Production Manager (UPM): The person responsible for managing production's costs.

Unity: Completeness of a work of literature. The key qualities in the construction of a plot, according to Aristotle, are: it has a beginning, middle, and end (i.e., is complete), and it is of appropriate size to be easily embraced in one view or easily embraced by memory.

Unity of Action: The cohesiveness that brings all the elements: conflict, crisis, characters, and action together.

Universality: A concept, need or emotion that can be related to by living things worldwide.

Unscripted: A line spoken or action taken during filming that was not in the original script.

Up: When the actor forgets their line during a rehearsal, they will indicate they are Up. *(Also known as Going Up)*

Up: The area toward the rear of the stage-away from the audience. *(Also known as Upstage)*

Upfronts: For networks, the preview of new shows for the upcoming season for advertisers.

Upgrade: Individuals being promoted to being a more significant part of the production. Or, a pay-rate increase, usually from extra status to principal status.

UPM: *See Unit Production Manager.*

Upping the Stakes: Increasing and upping the importance on a scene or moment to heighten the dramatic tension of the character or scene.

Upscale: The term refers to performers and extras that come in nicely dressed.

Upstage: Area of the stage farthest away from the auditorium that derives from the eighteenth century, when the stage was slanted, or raked toward the audience, with the rear of the stage higher than the front.

Upstage: An actor's attempt to distract audience attention from what another actor is doing. *(Also known as Up)*

Upstaging: To go upstage of an actor with whom you are sharing a scene. This causes the other actor to be in the downstage, a weakened position of having to face upstage to maintain the illusion of eye contact. Or, an actor's attempt to distract audience attention away from another actor.

UR: Abbreviation for Upstage Right. *(See Appendix: STAGE DIRECTION ABBREVIATIONS)*

URC: Abbreviation for Upstage Right Center. *(See Appendix: STAGE DIRECTION ABBREVIATIONS)*

URCS: Abbreviation for Upstage Right Center. *(See Appendix: STAGE DIRECTION ABBREVIATIONS)*

URS: Abbreviation for Upstage Right. *(See Appendix: STAGE DIRECTION ABBREVIATIONS)*

US: Abbreviation for Upstage. *(See Appendix: STAGE DIRECTION ABBREVIATIONS)*

Usage Fee: The practice of assigning each city in the US points based on population. An actors residuals on television or multimedia commercials are calculated based on the accumulation of these points in 13-week cycles.

USC: Abbreviation for Upstage Center. *(See Appendix: STAGE DIRECTION ABBREVIATIONS)*

USITT: *See The United States Institute of Theater Technology.*

USLC: Abbreviation for Upstage Left Center. *(See Appendix: STAGE DIRECTION ABBREVIATIONS)*

USR: Abbreviation for Upstage Right. *(See Appendix: STAGE DIRECTION ABBREVIATIONS)*

USRC: Abbreviation for Upstage Right Center. *(See Appendix: STAGE DIRECTION ABBREVIATIONS)*

V

Ventriloquist: A person who performs or is skilled in ventriloquism, the art of speaking, with little or no lip movement, so that the voice appears to come from another source, such as a wooden dummy.

Venue: The place where a performance is held.

Verbal Irony: Something different than what is said or the audience realizes.

Verisimilitude: The trait of seeming truthful or appearing to be real, from the Latin veri similis, meaning like the truth.

Versatility: The ability to change style or character with ease.

Verse: A line of metrical writing, a stanza, or a piece written in meter many times referred to as poetry. Or, the part of a song that precedes the chorus.

Vertical Sight Lines: Imaginary lines drawn from the highest seats of the audience area, often in a balcony, and from the seats in the front row, to the lowest hanging obstructions over the stage, to determine what portions of the performing area will be visible to all of the audience.

Vertigo Effect: An unsettling camera special effect that appears to undermine normal visual perception. A stationary object is filmed as the camera moves towards or away from it while adjusting its focal point so that the object remains the same size relative to the rest of the scene, accomplished by pulling the camera away from the focal object while zooming in at the same rate. Nicknamed the Vertigo Effect for famed writer/director/producer Alfred Hitchcock (1899-1980) who first used the special effect, conceived by Irmin Roberts, a second-unit cameraman, in his movie Vertigo. *(Also known as Contra-Zoom or Dolly Zoom or Hitchcock Zoom)*

Very Wide Shot (VWS): The subject is barely visible so the emphasis is still on placing the actor in their environment.

Vibrato: A natural wavering of frequency (pitch) while singing a note. It is usually inadvertent as opposed to a trill.

Video: The picture portion of a production. In film, it's called Picture.

Video Assist: A video feed coming directly from the camera lens which can be viewed on a monitor during shooting.

Video Toaster: A combination of hardware and software for the editing and production of video.

Video Village: The area where all of the camera shots are fed into video monitors, allowing the director to get an accurate view of every shot. Or, the encampment on the set around the video monitors so that all can view the action on set and not actually be on the set.

Viewpoints: A directing technique championed by Anne Bogart. Originally it was a dance and movement technique extended to apply to the movement of actors and manipulation of a stage image by a director. It was also later extended as an acting technique.

Villain: A performer who plays the negative or evil character in the storyline.

Vis, Visual Cue: A cue taken by a technician from the action on stage rather than being cued by the stage manager.

VOC: *See Voice On Camera.*

Vocal Coach: One who coaches singers, helping them with the pronunciation, singing and interpretation of a role.

Vocal Techniques: The three techniques to get the most out of dialogue, other than operative words, are visualize, physicalize, and structural embellishment.

Vocal Quality: The characteristics of a voice, such as shrill, nasal, raspy, breathy, booming, etc.

Voice on Camera: A scene where an actor speaks a line while the camera is on.

Voiceover (VO, V.O.): A term used to indicate off-camera directions, narration, commentary, etc.

Voice Over Edit: While a scene is played, another player steps forward and tells the audience what's next. The players in the scene stop whatever they're doing to make room for the voiceover. Once the voiceover is finished, the scene continues.

Volume: The degree of loudness or intensity of a voice.

VOM, Vomitorium: An entrance or exit to or from the stage through the house.

Voucher: Time slip with all pertinent information needed to get paid properly.

VWS: *See Very Wide Shot.*

W

W: Abbreviation for Working, an indication on a call sheet that means an actor is working on that day.

Waffling: Postponing by lack of ideas, while babbling in the hope of coming up with one.

Wagon: A movable platform, on wheels or air casters, used to carry scenery, props, or seating.

Wagon Stage: Mechanized stage where the scenery is moved into position on large sliding wagons as wide as the proscenium opening, from storage in large areas to the side and rear of the main stage. This system enables incredibly complex and otherwise time-consuming scene changes to occur almost instantly.

Waivers: A union's approval to deviate from the contract.

Walkaway: Break for meals when the cast and crew can go on their own to eat.

Walkdown: The time at the end of a stage performance when all the actors take their bows. *(Also known as Curtain Call)*

Walked It: Used critically for a lazy performance.

Walking Meal: Usually a second meal where the company doesn't actually stop filming, but food is provided.

Walk-On: For an extra, a non-speaking bit part. For a principal, a non-speaking entrance.

Walk Through: To perform a role at less-than-usual intensity, such as during a technical rehearsal. *(Also known as Camera Rehearsal)*

Walla Walla: The sound of many voices talking at once, such as at a party or in a restaurant, derived from saying "walla walla" over and over, which creates a good sound ambiance for a crowded scene.

Wallpaper Shot: Any shot that is used to fill the screen while a narrator is talking.

Wall-to-Wall: A series of unrelated scenes in an adult movie, with no plot.

Wardrobe: An actor's clothing for the performance or filming.

Wardrobe Allowance: Payment made to actors who use their own wardrobe during the filming.

Wardrobe Fitting: An appointment when actors are trying on wardrobe and costumes.

Wardrobe List: The list of clothes to wear for different styles of pictures.

Wardrobe Master/Mistress: The person in charge of the costume department.

Wardrobe Plot: Actor-by-actor, scene-by-scene inventory of all the costumes in a production, with a detailed breakdown into every separate item in each costume.

Warm-Up Person: A person who entertains the audience at a sitcom taping before the taping and between takes.

Warn Cue: Notification of an upcoming action or cue, usually indicated in the promptbook. *(Also known as Standby Cue)*

Wash: The whole acting area is evenly lit.

Weather Day: If the weather is not right for the shoot and it does not take place, it will be postponed. When this happens, the actor receives a half day's pay for each canceled day.

Weather Permit Call: During unplanned weather conditions, the production can dismiss actors four hours after call time.

Weather Shot: The subject is the weather and can be used for showing environment or setting mood or tone.

Wedge: A speaker that is angled so that it can sit on the stage floor and point up at performers.

Weekly Conversion: When an actor is converted from day player to freelance.

Weekly Player: Actor being paid on a weekly contract.

We're on the Wrong Set: What the AD says to signify a company's move to the next set or location.

Wet: A voice or sound with reverb or effects added to it. To record a sound without using any effect or other processing is known as dry.

Wet Paint Show: A production where all planning and thinking ahead have been put off to the last minute, thereby creating a sense of panic.

WGA: *See Writers Guild of America.*

What If: Acting tool invented by Konstantin Stanislavski where the actor asks, "What would I do if I were the character in the situation?" The ability to honestly place oneself in the situation and circumstances of a character through the use of emotional recall, sense memory, and imagination. *(Also known as Magic If)*

Whistle: Backstage whistles were originally used to instruct sailors who, because they knew the best knots, had the job of operating the theater's flying system. Whistling was forbidden otherwise backstage because it might result in a sailor cutting a rope and dropping something on somebody. The superstition of no whistling backstage is still in place. *(See Appendix: THEATER SUPERSTITIONS)*

White Noise: Random noise generated electronically, and covering the entire hearing spectrum.

White Space: The more white space each script page has means concise writing and breaks up action into smaller sections.

Wide Angle Lens: A lens which creates deep focus, increases the number of degrees visible, creates smaller image size, and hastens inward and outward movement.

Wide Shot (WS): Camera shot that is taken at a considerable distance from the subject, usually containing a large number of background objects. *(Also known as Long Shot)*

WIF: *See Women In Film.*

Wig Designer: Designs and oversees the creation of the wigs used in a production.

Wild Line: A single line from the script that is reread several times in succession until the perfect read is achieved. Wild lines are often done in a series. Or, lines that occur when the camera is on something other than you. They are wild because it is not necessary for them to be in sync with the actor's mouth.

Wild Sound: An audio recording synchronized with film or video, but recorded separately. *(Also known as Wild Track)*

Wild Spot: A commercial that runs on a non-network station, or a spot that runs on a network station but airs between scheduled programming.

Wild Track: An audio recording synchronized with film or video, but recorded separately. *(Also known as Wild Sound)*

Will-Notify: A call given to actors when call time is uncertain, indicates an actor will work, but no specific call time has been determined.

Wimped Out, Wimping: An improv term for not helping move the scene forward.

Window: The last shot of the day. *(Also known as Martini)*

Window Flat: Frames into which a window is built.

Windscreen, Windsock: A foam cover or fabric guard placed over a microphone to help prevent popped P's and other plosive sounds. *(Also known as Pop Filter)*

Wing and Drop Set: A set consisting of painted backdrop and accompanying painted wing curtains. When the location changes, both the backdrop and set of wings are flown out and replaced with another set, common in opera and ballet.

Wing It: To do something with in an impromptu manner, improvising, with little preparation.

Wings: The backstage or parts of a stage off to the left and right not seen by the audience.

Wip, Wipe: A transitional device where one image slowly replaces another by pushing the other out of the way.

Wipe: Single curtain moving across the stage on a single track (wipe track) rather than paired curtains on a tab track.

W/N: Abbreviation for Working No Time, an indication on a call sheet that an actor will be working on that particular day, but no time has been decided yet.

Women In Film (WIF): A professional organization committed to recognize, develop, and actively promote the unique visions of women in the global communications industry. *(See Appendix: ENTERTAINMENT INDUSTRY ASSOCIATIONS/ORGANIZATIONS)*

Woodshed: To rehearse or practice reading copy out loud.

Word-Perfect: Knowing perfectly one's dialogue, role, etc.

Working Blue: A style of performance, usually comedy, that is off-color, risqué, indecent or profane. *(Also known as Bathos or Blue or Blue Comedy or Blue Humor)*

Working Lights: High wattage lights used in a venue when the stage and auditorium lighting is not on. Used for rehearsals, fit-up, strike and resetting. Or, low wattage blue lights used to illuminate offstage obstacles and props tables, etc. *(Also known as Work Lights)*

Working Title: The temporary title of a project used during its development. *(Also known as Production Title)*

Work Lights: High wattage lights used in a venue when the stage/auditorium lighting is not on. Used for rehearsals, fit-up, strike and resetting. Or, low wattage blue lights used to illuminate offstage obstacles, etc. *(Also known as Working Lights)*

Work Permit: A legal document required to allow a child to work, issued by various state or local agencies.

Workshop: A place for putting together and polishing a production. Or, a session to receive instruction and practice in acting.

Work Vouchers: A paper given to an extra at the time of check-in. It must be filled out and turned in at the end of the day of shooting to receive wages.

World of the Play: The circumstances affected by the society, economics, culture and politics of the time. What we learn from the setting of the play, based on what happens, where it happens, and when it happens.

Wrangler: The person responsible for the younger cast members.

Wrap: The end of the filming for the day or for the whole production.

Wrap Party: Party that takes place after the production has finished.

Wrap Time: The hour the performer is finished working and able to leave set. This time will also include their time out of makeup and wardrobe.

Writer: Person who composes the script.

Writers Guild of America (WGA): The main organization for screenwriters in the US. *(See Appendix: ENTERTAINMENT INDUSTRY ASSOCIATIONS/ORGANIZATIONS)*

Writer's Signature: Unique style of the writer.

WS: *See Wide Shot.*

X

X: Abbreviation for 'crosses to' (e.g., Lead X armchair) in the prompt book.

XCU: *See Extreme Close Up*.

Xtra: Short for Extra, someone who acts in the background of a scene, with no dialogue, with the exception of repeatedly saying "rhubarb" or "walla" to mimic conversation.

Y

Yeller: Someone who yells their lines when not necessary or appropriate.

Yellow Jackets: Protective cable covers, for the safety of those on the set.

Yes And: Common method of advancing scenes, to accept everything said and/or done and do something with it. Also used as a verb, as in yes-anding.

Z

Zed Card: A modeling card, similar to a headshot, but is double-sided with four to five pictures showcasing different looks.

Zoom: A shot using a lens where the focal length is adjusted during the shot.

* * *

Bonus:
AWARDS PRESENTATIONS

The following is a listing of the 30 most popular American entertainment awards shows and presentations.

Academy Awards/Oscars:. The first Academy Awards were held in 1929 in the Hollywood Roosevelt Hotel and have been televised since 1953. The Oscars honor achievements in film, generally considered the most important awards in Hollywood.

Academy of Country Music Awards/ACM: First held in 1966, it was the first country music awards program held by a major organization, and first televised in 1972.

ACE Eddie Awards: Beginning in 1950, the American Cinema Editors honored the film editing Academy Award nominees, but now celebrates the best in TV, multimedia, and feature film editing.

American Music Awards: Created by Dick Clark in 1973 for ABC when the network's contract to air the Grammy Awards expired. The AMA's are determined by the public who vote through online.

Art Directors Guild Awards: For excellence in art direction for films, TV, multimedia, commercials and music videos, voted on by the International Alliance of Theatrical and Stage Employees.

BET Awards: Established in 2001 by the Black Entertainment Television network to celebrate African Americans and other minorities in music, acting, sports, and other fields of entertainment.

Billboard Music Awards: Given by Billboard, which tracks music popularity. The awards show was held annually since 1989, until it went dormant in 2006, but returned in 2011.

CMT Awards: A fan-voted awards show for country music videos and television or multimedia performances. The awards ceremony is held every year in Nashville, Tennessee.

Costume Designers Guild Awards: Founded in 1953, its international membership recognizes excellence in costume design in film, television, multimedia, and commercials.

Critics' Choice Movie Awards: Formerly known as the Broadcast Film Critics Association Awards, these are presented by the Broadcast Film Critics Association/BFCA to honor the finest in cinematic achievement.

Critics' Choice Awards: Presented by the Coks Broadcast Television Journalists Association. Established in 2011, the first ceremony was streamed live on VH1.com.

Directors Guild Awards: Started in 1948 by George Marshall, the President of the Screen Directors Guild, which became the Directors Guild of America, Inc. in 1960, these awards now include directorial achievement in film, television, multimedia, and commercials.

Emmy Awards - Daytime: An accolade bestowed by the National Academy of Television Arts and Sciences in recognition of excellence in American daytime television and web-based programming.

Emmy Awards - Primetime: Recognizes excellence in American primetime television programming, these were first given in 1949. They are considered the television equivalent to the Academy Awards (film), Grammy Awards (music), and Tony Awards (stage).

Film Independent Spirit Awards: Honoring arts-driven films made on independent-level budgets in 15 categories.

Golden Globe Awards: First held in 1947 to honor achievements in film, television, and multimedia. Voting is by members of the Hollywood Foreign Press Association who are journalists that cover the entertainment industry for outlets around the world.

Golden Raspberry Awards: Also known as the Razzies, these annually celebrate the worst in film and considered the anti-Oscars,. Anyone who pays for a Razzie membership can vote.

Grammy Awards: Presented by the Recording Academy, the Grammys celebrate achievement in the recording arts and are meant to determine winners based on artistic and technical merit.

Kennedy Center Honors: An annual honor given to those in the performing arts for their lifetime contributions to American culture, presented annually since 1978 in the Kennedy Center Opera House.

Kids' Choice Awards: The KCA's air on the Nickelodeon cable channel, and honor the year's biggest television, movie, and music acts, as voted by Nickelodeon viewers. Winners receive a hollow orange blimp figurine, which also functions as a kaleidoscope.

Latin Grammy Awards: Given by The Latin Academy of Recording Arts & Sciences, these honor works produced anywhere around the world that were recorded in either Spanish or Portuguese.

MTV Movie Awards: Presented annually on MTV, the nominees are decided by producers and executives at MTV, but winners are decided on MTV's website by the general public, and winners are presented with a golden popcorn statue.

MTV Video Music Awards/VMA: Presented by MTV to present these video music awards, the VMA's were originally the alternative to the Grammy Awards in the video category. The statue given to winners is an astronaut on the moon, called a Moon Person.

Peabody Awards/George Foster Peabody Awards: Named for American businessman and philanthropist George Foster Peabody, these recognize public service by radio and television stations, networks, online media, producing organizations, and individuals.

People's Choice Awards: Founded in 1975 to give fans a chance to express their opinions about pop culture. Decided by an online public vote, these honor film, TV, multimedia, and music in 58 categories.

Producers Guild of America Awards: Originally established in 1990 as the Golden Laurel Awards to honor the visionaries who produce and execute film, television, and multimedia product.

Screen Actors Guild Awards: Given since 1995, and now honoring acting in film, television, and multimedia, the top awards go to ensemble casts in to highlight collaborative acting. The nude male statuette holding masks of comedy and tragedy, is called The Actor.

Teen Choice Awards: The awards honor the year's biggest achievements in music, movies, sports, television, fashion, and more, voted on by kids aged 10-15. The award is a custom-made surfboard to represent the freedom of summer vacation.

Tony Awards:.Founded in 1947, The Antoinette Perry Award for Excellence in Theater award recognizes achievement in live Broadway theater. The face of the Tony Award medallion portrays an adaptation of the comedy and tragedy masks.

Writers Guild of America Awards: Since 1949, awards outstanding writing achievements in film, television, radio, and video game writing, and includes both fiction and non-fiction categories.

* * *

Appendix I:
ENTERTAINMENT INDUSTRY ASSOCIATONS/ORGANIZATIONS

The entertainment industry, or those involved in providing entertainment in film, multimedia, television, and theater, have a variety of industry organizations. This is but a partial list of the multitude of associations and organizations available for membership.

1. **Academy of Motion Picture Arts and Sciences (AMPAS):** One of the world's preeminent movie-related organizations, with a membership of more than 6,000.
2. **Academy of Television Arts and Sciences (ATAS):** A nonprofit organization devoted to the advancement of arts and sciences.
3. **Actors Equity Association/Equity (AEA):** Equity negotiates wages, working conditions, and provides a range of benefits, including health and pension plans.
4. **The Actors Fund:** A nonprofit charitable organization that assists American performing arts professionals through a spectrum of programs.
5. **American Association of Actors and Artistes (4A's):** A member of the AFL-CIO and a few of the individual unions are not. This distinction is purely technical as the 4As splits its votes in AFL-CIO elections based on the wishes of each member union. The current AAAA member unions of the AFL-CIO are: AEA, AGMA, GIAA, and SAG-AFTRA.
6. **American Cinema Editors (ACE):** An honorary society of film editors that are voted in based on the qualities of professional achievements, their education of others, and their dedication to editing.
7. **American Federation of Musicians of the United States and Canada (AFM):** The largest organization of musicians in the world, with more than 80,000 musicians who perform in orchestras, backup bands, festivals, clubs and theaters, both on Broadway and on tour. AFM members also make music for films, television, multimedia, commercials and sound recordings.

8. **American Film Institute (AFI):** Dedicated to advancing and preserving the art of the moving image.
9. **Association of Talent Agents (ATA):** A nonprofit trade association composed of companies engaged in the talent agency business.
10. **Casting Society of America (CSA):** A professional organization of casting directors working in theater, film, television, and multimedia. CSA is not a union or a guild, therefore every casting director working is not necessarily a member of this organization.
11. **Directors Guild of America (DGA):** An entertainment organization that represents the interests of film and television directors in the United States.
12. **Dramatists Guild of America (DG):** The professional organization of playwrights composers and lyricists, based in New York.
13. **The Film Foundation (TFF):** Educates the public about the importance of protecting and preserving film art; defends artists' work threatened with modification or distortion; and promotes public debate about these issues to help safeguard our intellectual and cultural heritage.
14. **International Federation of Actors (FIA):** A global federation of performers' trade unions, guilds and professional associations. Founded in 1952, it represents several hundreds of thousands of performers with some 90 member organizations in more than 60 countries around the world.
15. **League Of Resident Theatres (LORT):** The largest professional theater association of its kind in the United States and issues contracts with Actor's Equity regarding the payment and treatment of actors.
16. **A Minor Consideration (AMC):** Addresses the concerns of children in the industry.
17. **Motion Picture & Television Fund (MPTF):** Supports the entertainment community in living and aging well, with dignity and purpose, and in helping each other in times of need.
18. **Motion Picture Association of America (MPAA):** The voice and advocate of the American motion picture industry.

19. **National Endowment for the Arts (NEA):** Established by Congress in 1965 to support artistic excellence, creativity, and innovation for the benefit of individuals and communities through partnerships with state arts agencies, local leaders, other federal agencies, and the philanthropic sector.

20. **NewFilmmakers Los Angeles (NFMLA):** A non-profit organization championing independent filmmakers worldwide. The festival provides a forum where filmmakers can be recognized for their accomplishments, gain exposure to new audiences, and connect with industry professionals for insight on distribution, production, acquisition, and representation.

21. **Recording Industry Association of America (RIAA):** A trade organization that represents the recording industry in the United States, whose members consist of record labels and distributors.

22. **Screen Actors Guild Foundation (SAG-AFTRA):** Provides vital assistance and educational programming to its members while serving the public at large through its signature children's literacy programs.

23. **United States Institute for Theater Technology (USITT):** A nonprofit serving the performing arts design, theater tech and production fields.

24. **Women In Film (WIF):** A professional organization committed to recognize, develop, and actively promote the unique visions of women in the communications industry.

25. **Writers Guild of America (WGA):** The main organization for screenwriters in the US.

* * *

Appendix II:
THEATER SUPERSTITIONS

Theater is filled with superstitions and traditions that have been passed down from generation to generation. The following is a list of the 10 most popular superstitions.

1. **Superstition: It is bad luck to say "good luck" to an actor.** Some performers believe there are ghosts who make the opposite of what you say occur.
2. **Superstition: No whistling in the theater.** In the 1600s, whistling was a common signal to move scenery, causing dangerous confusion if others whistled. The whistling has stopped, but the tradition continues.
3. **Superstition: Avoid placing a peacock feather onstage.** The pattern on a peacock feather creates, according to Ancient Greek legend, an evil eye, which brings bad luck.
4. **Superstition: Turn on a ghost light.** Theaters, lit by gas, ran a ghost light flame, eliminating explosive pressure. Some still believe a light helps keep spirits away.
5. **Superstition: Do not give flowers before the performance.** Flowers should only be given to performers after a show. To do so before ensures a bad performance.
6. **Superstition: Ban blue onstage.** Long ago, a theater troupe's success was judged by its ability to afford blue costumes. Still considered unlucky, but ok with silver.
7. **Superstition: A bad dress rehearsal means a great opening night.** It is more likely that a bad dress rehearsal is the result of a tired cast and crew whereas the opening night audience reinvigorates the performers.
8. **Superstition: Unlucky rule of three.** Having three lit candles onstage is bad luck. The person nearest to the shortest candle will be the next to marry, or die.
9. **Superstition: No mirrors on stage.** Many believe that mirrors are a reflection of the soul and breaking one can mean seven years bad luck for the theater itself.
10. **Superstition: Never say "Macbeth" in a theater.** The actor playing Macbeth in the original show died. If you say "Macbeth" you must go outside, spin 3 times and spit.

***

Appendix III:
STAGE DIRECTION ABBREVIATIONS

BACKSTAGE

STAGE RIGHT   **STAGE LEFT**

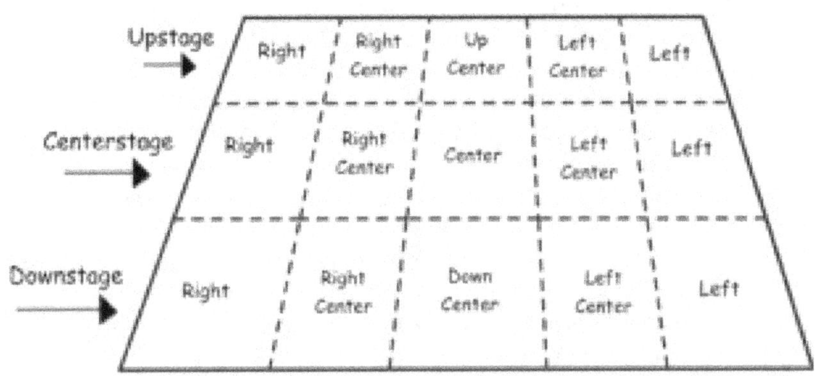

HOUSE LEFT   **HOUSE RIGHT**
AUDIENCE

C, CS: Centerstage
D, DS: Downstage
DC, DCS, DSC: Downstage Center
DLC, DLCS, DSLC: Downstage Left Center
DL, DLS, DSL: Downstage Left
DR, DRS, DSR: Downstage Right
DRC, DRCS, DSRC: Downstage Right Center
HL: House Left
HR: House Right
L, LS: Left Stage

LC, LCS: Left Center Stage
R, RS: Right Stage
RC, RCS: Right Center Stage
SL: Stage Left
SR: Stage Right
U, US: Upstage
UC, UCS, USC: Upstage Center
UL, ULS, USL: Upstage Left
ULC, ULCS, USLC: Upstage Left Center
UR, URS, USR: Upstage Right
URC, URCS, USRC: Upstage Right Center

* * *

Appendix IV:
PERFORMING ARTS GENRES

These are the most popular film, serial, and specialty genres, noting that some of these genres can be combined, and most have further sub-categories.

FILM GENRES

Most films are singular, but others have sequels that continue or develop the theme of an earlier one.

1. **Action:** The protagonist has a series of challenges that typically include physical feats, high-speed chases, and violence.
2. **Adult:** Uses graphic nudity and a sexually explicit plot line.
3. **Adventure:** The protagonist journeys to epic or distant places to accomplish something.
4. **Avante-Garde/Experimental:** Radical or unorthodox with respect to society.
5. **Children/Teens:** For smaller children, usually colorful animation, For pre-teens or teens, usually includes several co-leads suffering through teenage angst.
6. **Comedy:** A series of funny or comical events, intended to make the audience laugh.
7. **Crime:** A crime that is being committed, or was committed, or an account of a criminal's life.
8. **Drama:** Fiction, or semi-fiction, intended to be serious, focusing on characters who must deal with realistic emotional struggles.
9. **Documentary:** Non-fiction, intended to document reality for the purposes of instruction or maintaining a historical record.
10. **Epic:** A historical or imagined person or event, with an extravagant setting, lavish costumes, and a sweeping musical score, and often covers a large expanse of time.
11. **Family:** A humorous plot line, intended to appeal to people of any age, with a family or several co-lead characters.

12. **Historical:** A real person or event that happened in the past.
13. **Horror:** Deliberately scares or frightens, through suspense, violence or shock.
14. **Musical:** Integrates full-scale scores and choreographed dance routines.
15. **Mystery:** Follows the protagonist, who usually portrays an investigator, as they attempt to solve a puzzle, most often a crime.
16. **Romance:** Emotion-driven, primarily focused on the relationship between the main characters, usually with a happy ending.
17. **Science Fiction/Fantasy:** Surreal plot line that challenges rational reasoning, usually by way of magic or supernatural forces.
18. **Thriller:** Dark or serious theme that is usually a mix of fear and excitement, with traits from action, adventure, mystery, or horror genres.
19. **War:** Acknowledges the horror and heartbreak of war, using actual combat fighting as the primary plot or background for the action.
20. **Western:** Dedicated to the early days of the expansion of the American frontier.

SERIAL GENRES

Broadcast in several separate parts, these series usually deal with the same subject or have the same hosts or characters.

1. **Animal:** Shows how different types of animals live, both domestically and in the wild.
2. **Animation:** Features cartoon characters, and can be child or adult-themed.
3. **Children:** Geared towards kids of all ages, these can be educational or strictly for amusement.
4. **Anthology:** Presents a different story and set of characters in each episode, usually with a different cast, but may use a permanent group of actors who appear in a different drama after a storyline is complete.
5. **Comedy:** Consists of jokes (as in stand-up), or satirical short segments (as in sketch), or the same characters in different situations (as in sitcom), to invoke laughter.

6. **Court:** Presents content in the form of legal hearings between plaintiffs and defendants, presided over by a pseudo-judge.
7. **Current Affairs:** Shows detailed analysis and discussion of news stories that have recently occurred or are ongoing.
8. **Instructional (DIY/Do-It-Yourself):** Shows and usually teaches people how to grow, cook repair, or make or do things on their own.
9. **Docudrama:** A dramatization based on real events.
10. **Documentary:** Intended to document reality, primarily for the purposes of instruction, education, or maintaining a historical record.
11. **Drama:** A fiction, or semi-fiction storyline, intended to be serious, focusing on characters who deal with realistic emotional struggles.
12. **Game Show Competitions:** People compete with each other or the game itself by answering questions, challenging each other's athleticism, or playing games to win prizes.
13. **Music:** Features live or recorded music.
14. **News:** Delivers noteworthy information, especially about recent or important events.
15. **Newsmagazine:** Features in-depth short segments, combining interviews, commentary, and entertainment, and usually focuses on human interest stories.
16. **Public Affairs:** Focuses on matters of politics and public policy.
17. **Reality Show:** People showing what they do in their day-to-day life, or in staged situations, or people helping other people change their image.
18. **Religious:** Usually produced by religious organizations, with a religious message.
19. Shopping: Where people can either buy featured items or bid for them.
20. **Soap Opera:** Examines the lives of many characters, usually focusing on emotional relationships to the point of melodrama. (Another Latin American term for this that is gaining popularity in the US is Telenovela.)
21. **Sports:** Features sports competition, commentary, or sporting events.

22. **Talk:** Usually hosted by a celebrity, these feature guests who are either other celebrities that talk about their lives, or experts who talk about topics such as fashion, health and leisure.
23. **Travel:** Features popular travel destinations or reviews.
24. **Variety:** Includes a variety of acts, especially musical performances and sketch comedy, and normally introduced by a host.

SPECIALTY GENRES

These are broadcast on an occasional, annual, or as-needed basis.

1. **Awards:** A formal program where prizes are given to honor achievement in a particular field.
2. **Charity:** Usually a variety or music program that aims to raise funds for charity or relief by persuading people to donate money.
3. **Commercial:** A short-form advertisement, usually 15-60 seconds, produced and paid for by an organization or company, typically to market a product or service.
4. **Holiday:** Features holiday themes and music, usually in a variety format.
5. **Infomercial:** A long-form advertisement, usually 15-30 minutes, that generally includes contact information to directly sell a product.
6. **Miniseries:** Tells a story, usually an epic drama, in a limited number of episodes.
7. **Variety:** Includes a variety of acts, especially musical performances and sketch comedy, and normally introduced by a host.

* * *

Appendix V:
CAMERA SHOTS

The amount of space seen in one shot or frame, used to show different aspects of characters, settings, and themes. The following is a list of 65 common shot types, along with a brief description of each.

1. **Aerial Shot:** A shot taken from a crane, plane, or helicopter, but not necessarily a moving shot.
2. **American Shot:** From the westerns of the 1930-40s to show the actor's gun holsters, it frames from mid-thighs up. *(Also known as Cowboy Shot)*
3. **American Two Shot:** A shot that shows the two heads facing each other in profile to the camera.
4. **Arc Shot:** A shot where a moving camera circles around the subject.
5. **Beauty Shot:** The last shot on a television or multimedia show, used to run the credits, or one that emphasizes something's attractive aspects.
6. **Big Head Close Up Shot:** A shot that includes the eyes and mouth, but not the whole head.
7. **Bird's-Eye View Shot:** Taken from directly overhead and from a distance, often from on a crane or helicopter. (Also known as Top Shot)
8. **Bridging Shot:** A shot used to cover a jump in time or place, or other discontinuity, such as falling calendar pages or seasons changing.
9. **Choker Shot:** Frames the actor's face from just below the mouth to just above the eyebrows.
10. **Close-Up Shot:** Fills the screen with part of the actor, such as the actor's face or head.
11. **Cowboy Shot:** From the westerns of the 1930-40s to show the actor's gun holsters, it frames from mid-thighs up. *(Also known as American Shot)*
12. **Crane Shot:** Taken from a device resembling a extendable mechanical arm that can raise the camera up, providing an overhead view of a scene.

13. **Crowd Shot:** Shows a large group of people, however CGI is now often used to film very large crowd shots to avoid huge costs associated with hiring extras.
14. **Cutaway Shot:** A shot of something specific, other than the actors, and away from the main scene.
15. **Cut-In Shot:** Similar to a cutaway, but shows a close-up shot of something visible in the main scene.
16. **Distance Shot:** Used to show the actors or location from a distance, useful for establishing a scene. *(Also known as Extreme Long Shot or Extreme Wide Shot)*
17. **Dolly Shot:** A moving camera shot that uses a wheeled camera platform known as a dolly.
18. **Dolly Zoom Shot:** The foreground stays the same, while the background increases as the camera tracks forward while zooming out, or vice-versa.
19. **Dutch Angle Shot:** The camera is set at an angle so the horizon line is not level, used to show a disoriented psychological state. *(Also known as Tilt Shot)*
20. **Establishing Shot:** Usually used in the first scene to establish mood, location, environment, and era, and usually long or extreme long shots.
21. **Extreme Close Up Shot:** Emphasizes a small area or detail of the actor, such as the hands or mouth, or of the eyes. *(Also known as Italian Shot)*
22. **Extreme Long Shot:** Used to show the actors or location from a large distance. *(Also known as Distance Shot or Extreme Wide Shot)*
23. **Extreme Wide Shot:** Used to show the actors or location from a distance. *(Also known as Distance Shot or Extreme Long Shot)*
24. **Eye Level Shot:** Shot taken with the camera at human eye level, resulting in a neutral effect on the audience.
25. **Follow Shot:** A tracking, zoom shot that follows the subject as it moves.
26. **Full Shot:** Fills the frame with the actor from head to toe, with the emphasis more on action and movement rather than a character's emotional state.
27. **Group Shot:** Shows a large group of people. *(Also known as Crowd Shot)*

28. **Head and Shoulder Shot:** The standard shot when there are two subjects engaged in conversation, which frames a person from the chest up.

29. **High Angle Shot:** From above eye level, this shot can have the effect of making the character seem weak or frightened.

30. **Inserts Shot:** Tiny sections of close-up action used to illustrate specific points, such as a finger dialing a telephone, which would get lost in a wider view.

31. **Introductory Shot:** When a sequence of the subject is shot doing other things and added to the final video, it makes the person seem more interesting.

32. **Italian Shot:** Emphasizes a small area or detail of the actor, such as the hands or mouth, or of the eyes. *(Also known as Extreme Close Up Shot)*

33. **Jump Cut Shot:** Two shots that follow each other but don't follow the logical order of the story, or don't make apparent sense.

34. **Long Shot:** Still dominated by the environment, but the character becomes more of a focus than in an extreme long shot. *(Also known as Wide Shot)*

35. **Low Angle Shot:** From below eye level, this shot can have the effect of making the character seem powerful or dangerous.

36. **Martini Shot:** The last shot of the day. *(Also known as Window Shot)*

37. **Master Shot:** A single, uninterrupted shot of a scene which may be the only shot, or edited together with additional shots including multiple shot types.

38. **Medium Close-Up Shot:** Falls between a medium shot and a close-up, generally framing the actor from chest or shoulder up.

39. **Medium Long Shot:** Between a full shot and a medium shot, this one usually shows the actor from the knees up, sometimes known as a 3/4 shot.

40. **Medium Shot:** The most common shot used in the industry, shot from the waist up, it focuses on the actor while still showing some environment.

41. **Medium Two Shot :** This shot frames two people in a medium shot and can be expanded to a medium three shot, four shot, etc.

42. **Noddy Shot:** This shot is used in recorded news or interviews to show the interviewer nodding or exhibiting other similar listening gestures.

43. **Over-the-Shoulder Shot:** From behind the shoulder of another actor, this shot frames the actor speaking, while still showing the back of the other one.

44. **Panning Shot:** Movement of the camera from left to right or right to left around an imaginary vertical axis. *(Also known as Panoramic Shot)*

45. **Panoramic Shot:** Movement of the camera from left to right or right to left around an imaginary vertical axis. *(Also known as Panning Shot)*

46. **Point of View Shot:** Intended to show what a particular character is seeing, such as looking through a periscope or binoculars.

47. **Pull Back Shot:** A tracking or zoom shot that moves back from the subject to reveal the context of the scene.

48. **Reaction Shot:** This shows a character's reaction to the shot that has just preceded it.

49. **Reverse Angle Shot:** A camera shot set up to shoot the reverse 180° view of the previous shot, commonly used during conversation.

50. **Three Quarter Shot:** A variation between the medium and full shot, this one frames a person from the knees up.

51. **Tight Cowboy Shot:** This shot frames the actor from above the guns holstered on the hips, originating from the westerns of the 1930-40s.

52. **Tight-On Shot:** A shot that focuses on a single subject and allows for very little to no extra space around. *(Also known as Tight Shot)*

53. **Tight Shot:** A shot that focuses on a single subject and allows for very little to no extra space around. *(Also known as Tight-On Shot)*

54. **Tilt Shot:** The camera is set at an angle so the horizon line is not level, often used to show a disoriented psychological state. *(Also known as Dutch Angle Shot)*

55. **Top Shot:** Taken from directly overhead from a distance, often from on a crane or helicopter.

56. **Tracking Shot:** A shot where the camera is moved by means of wheels, such as a dolly, a car, a train, etc. *(Also known as Traveling Shot)*

57. **Traveling Shot:** The camera is moved on a track or by means of wheels, such as a dolly, a car, a train, etc. *(Also known as Tracking Shot)*

58. **Two-Shot (Three, Four, Etc.):** Designates how many actors appear in the shot. The one or two-shot are the most commonly ones used.

59. **Two Shot West:** One actor turns 180° to face away from the other one while they continue to talk, allowing both to appear facing the camera.

60. **Very Wide Shot**: The subject is barely visible so the emphasis is still on placing the actor in their environment.

61. **Wallpaper Shot:** Any shot that is used to fill the screen while a narrator is talking.

62. **Weather Shot:** The subject is the weather and can be used for showing environment or setting mood or tone.

63. **Wide Shot:** This shows the whole scene, used to establish the location or setting and can also be used to introduce action. *(Also known as Long Shot)*

64. **Window Shot:** The last shot of the day. *(Also known as Martini Shot)*

65. **Zoom Shot:** A shot using a lens where the focal length is adjusted during the shot.

* * *

Appendix VI:
SCRIPT ABBREVIATIONS

The following is a list of 70 common script abbreviations.

1. **2-S or 3-S, etc.:** two shot, etc.
2. **2-SHOT or 3-SHOT, etc.:** two shot, three shot, etc.
3. **3/4:** three quarter shot
4. **ANG:** angle
5. **ANNCR:** announcer
6. **b.g., Bg, BG:** background
7. **BCU, BH/CU:** big head close-up
8. **CG:** character generation
9. **CH/SH:** chocker shot
10. **CL:** camera left
11. **COMP:** complete
12. **CONT:** continued
13. **CR:** camera right
14. **CS:** close shot
15. **CU:** close-up
16. **D/A:** down angle
17. **DBLE:** double
18. **D/I:** dolly in
19. **DIAL:** dialogue
20. **DIS, DISS:** dissolve
21. **ECU:** extreme close-up
22. **ELS:** extreme long shot
23. **ENT:** enter
24. **EST, ESTB:** establishing shot
25. **eu:** close-up
26. **EXT:** exterior
27. **F2/SH, F3/SH, etc.:** full two shot, full three shot, etc.
28. **f.g., Fg, FG:** foreground
29. **F/I:** fade in
30. **F/O:** fade out
31. **FS, F/SH:** full shot
32. **FT:** feet
33. **F/X:** special effects
34. **GR/SH:** group shot
35. **H/A:** high angle
36. **H&S:** head and shoulders shot
37. **INC:** incomplete
38. **INT:** interior
39. **L/A:** low angle
40. **L-R:** left to right
41. **LS, L/SH:** long shot
42. **LWR:** lower-screen position
43. **MCU:** medium close-up
44. **MIC:** microphone
45. **MID:** mid-screen position
46. **MLS:** medium long shot
47. **MO:** music over
48. **MS:** medium shot
49. **O.C.:** off camera
50. **OS, O/S:** over-the-shoulder shot
51. **O.S.:** off screen
52. **OSV:** off-screen voice
53. **OVS:** over-the-shoulder shot
54. **POV:** point of view shot
55. **P.O.V.:** point of view
56. **Q:** cue—as in cue talent
57. **SND EFX:** sound effects
58. **SFX:** special effects—sound/visual
59. **SOF:** sound on film
60. **SOT:** sound on tape
61. **SUPER:** superimposition
62. **UPR:** upper-screen position
63. **VO/V.O.:** voiceover
64. **VWS:** very wide shot
65. **WS:** wide shot
66. **X:** crosses over to
67. **XCU:** extreme close up shot
68. **X/S:** over-the-shoulder shot
69. **ZI:** zoom in
70. **ZO:** zoom out

* * *

Appendix VII:
SPEC SCRIPT EXAMPLE

A spec script is written without camera directions
or scene numbers, with 12pt Courier font.

FADE IN:

INT. CLINIC - EXAM ROOM - DAY

VANESSA SMITH, 70s, puts a hat on her
bald head after an exam.

Sitting with her is her DOCTOR. He hands
Vanessa a prescription.

                DOCTOR
        I'm giving you stronger pain
        medication.

                VANESSA
        Tell me the truth. How long?

                DOCTOR
        Two, maybe three months.

                VANESSA
        Will the headaches get worse?

                DOCTOR
        It's hard to tell.

                (CONTINUED)

                    DOCTOR
                    (CON'T)
          This new medication should
          help.

INT. BAR - DAY

Vanessa at the bar with ZACH, 60s, a
friend.

                    ZACH
                  (tearing up)
          That's terrible news!

                    VANESSA
          I know, but it's been a good
          life. No crying allowed.

                              FADE OUT.

Spec Script Writing Software:

Final Draft — the industry leader
SoCreate — an industry newcomer
Celtx — a bare-bones free option

                  ***

Appendix VIII:
SHOOTING SCRIPT EXAMPLES

The script as prepared for shooting, marked with directives and the scenes numbered consecutively. There are many stages of shooting scripts, including ones with handwritten notes as changes are made, and scripts with changes indicated on a page by a new page or text color.

EXAMPLE #1: This is page one of the Raging Bull shooting script with notes. Lead actor Robert De Niro's notes mention props, costumes, motivations and fight techniques, with comments such as, "always find ways to express self thru body," and specific references to the fight in the opening scene.

Image courtesy of The Robert De Niro Collection at the University of Texas at Austin

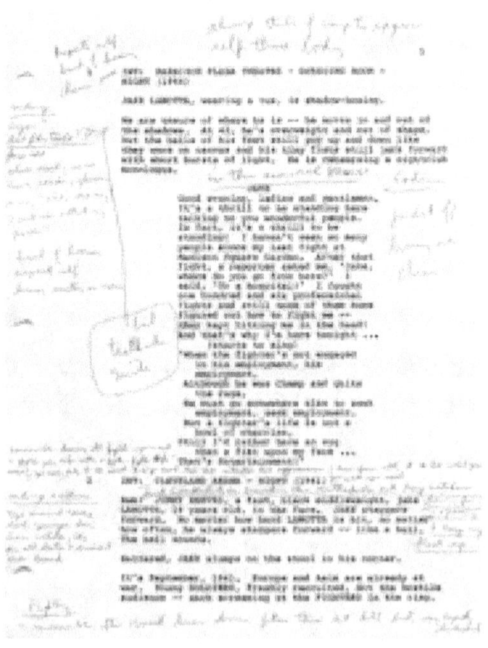

EXAMPLE #2: A lined shooting script is marked up by the director to indicate when and where there will be camera coverage. Basic information such as the shot number, shot size, and amount of coverage is indicated very simply by using short form notes.

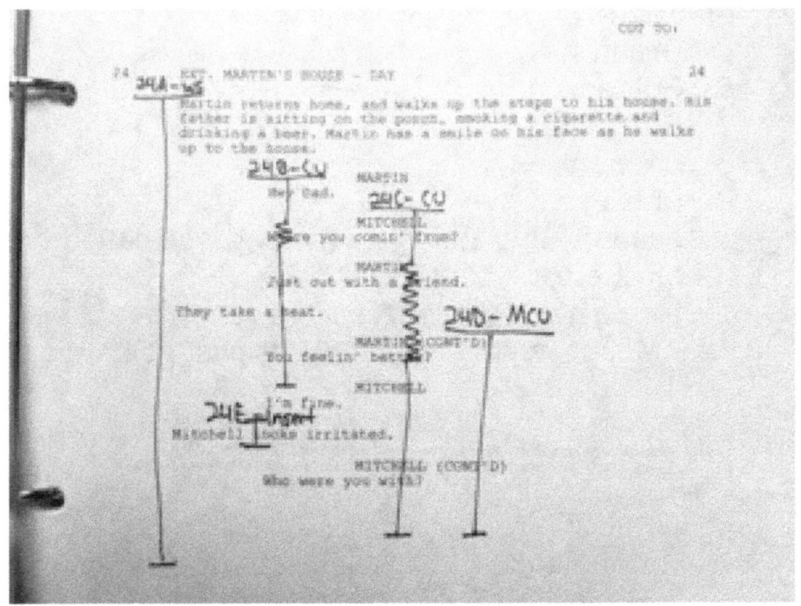

*Image courtesy of **normkroll.com***

EXAMPLE #3: A production shooting script indicates changes by a new page or text color, or the color name written on the top of the page According to the WGA west, the standard script revision colors are:

1. White (unrevised)
2. Blue
3. Pink
4. Yellow
5. Green
6. Goldenrod*
7. Buff
8. Salmon
9. Cherry
10. Second Blue Revision (sometimes called double blue, etc.)
11. Second Pink Revision and so on...
    *Most scripts never make it past goldenrod.

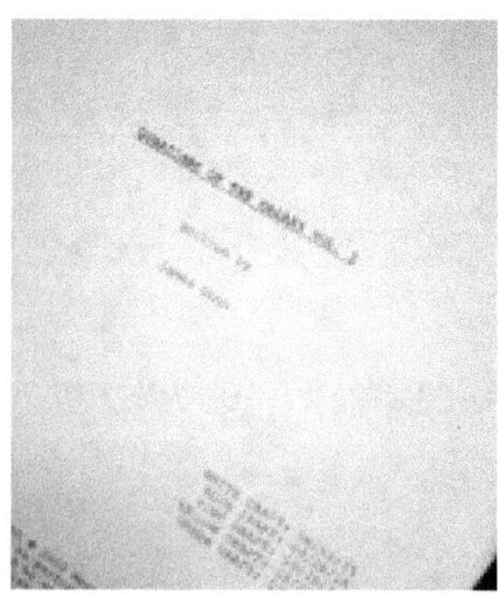

*Image courtesy of **http://screenwriting.jo***

* * *

Appendix IX:
ACTOR'S RESUME

An actor's resume is the tool used to obtain an agent or a role, and includes an actor's information, including credits, personal details, special skills, etc. There is no one exact format, but there are certain items that should be included and standards that should be met. Many sample templates can be found online. The following are the 10 things necessary to create an effective actor's resume:

1. The resume should be one page only and must fit on the back of an 8x10 headshot. It is acceptable to staple the resume to the back of your headshot as opposed to print directly onto it, since the resume may change frequently.
2. Use black ink with an easy to read font, such as Arial.
3. Your name in large bold letters followed by your contact information, including telephone number and email address, height, weight, hair color, and eye color at the top, but leave out personal home address information.
4. Union associations are also included at the top portion of the resume.
5. In the center section, list the credits or roles you've had in plays, musicals, films, television, multimedia shows, commercials, voiceovers, etc. Put each in its own category, even if there's only one entry. And, don't add credits that are too old unless that's all you have.
6. Include the training you've received, such as where you studied and what kind of program it was.
7. List any special skills you have, such as singing, playing an instrument, speaking a foreign language, etc.
8. Let them know what type(s) you associate yourself with: intellect, bombshell, romantic lead, funnyman, girl next door, character, etc.
9. Remember, less is more. Leave enough white space on the resume so it's easy to read.
10. **DO NOT LIE**...you will get caught, and word will spread, making it difficult to find work.

* * *

Appendix X:
TIPS TO FINDING AN AGENT, SURVIVING AN INTERVIEW, GETTING AN AUDITION, AND LANDING THE PART

The goal is to land the part, but first you must land the audition. You can do it without representation, or you can find an agent and/or manager who will help find auditions for you, and may have access to auditions you'll never even hear about otherwise.

FINDING AUDITIONS ON YOUR OWN
1. **Use your own contacts.** Ask your acting teachers, colleagues and friends if they know of any upcoming projects in your area.
2. **Try out some casting calls.** You can find them in your local newspapers, websites, television, multimedia, radios and elsewhere.
3. **Use social media.** Facebook, Twitter, and Craigslist are all great resources for getting auditions. Event pages are often used to announce open casting calls and auditions.
4. **Look at agents' Facebook pages.** Sometimes, audition and contact information is there.
5. **Create an account on audition websites.** Some examples of these include www.exploretalent.com, www.laauditions.com, www.actoraccess.com, or www.backstage.com.
6. **Contact your local film office.** Most films that are looking for extras will advertise through your city's film office and will also have a list of current projects, permits and contacts.

FINDING AN AGENT OR MANAGER

1. **Ask for a reference.** If you have friends, colleagues, or classmates with agents, ask them to pass along your information. Give them copies of your headshot, resume, and reel to pass along.
2. **Find a local community of actors.** Get to know them. They can help you get your reel and headshot to the right person.
3. **Act in plays or local films/commercials.** Even if it volunteer or low paying, or part of your school activities. You might get noticed by an agent.
4. **Find contacts through social media.** Facebook, Twitter, and Youtube can give you amazing exposure through friend and business networks.
5. **Go to an agent workshop.** Agents sometimes hold these to find new talent. Make sure you look professional and unique. First impressions are key in the film and theater industry.
6. **Get a meeting with an agent.** Once you've made a contact and you get to know an agent, it is best to set up a formal meeting.

INTERVIEW DO'S AND DON'TS

1. **DO make sure your resume and headshots are current.** Make sure it highlights all your acting experience. And, no one wants to see what you looked like five years ago.
2. **DO your research.** Learn all you can about the person or company that is interviewing you. Sharing that knowledge will give you an edge and shows you have the research skills necessary to study future parts you will play.
3. **DO be professional with a confident attitude.** Dress in business attire and stay away from any costume-like clothing. Rehearse talking to the interviewers with an energetic voice and actively listen so that you can carry on an intelligent conversation.

4. **DO NOT talk too much.** Answer questions concisely and leave out any information about personal, health, relationship or financial problems. In addition, do not be overly personal, which can raise red flags about your ability to be appropriate later.

5. **DO NOT complain.** No matter how horrible your previous role was, keep it to yourself. Constant negativity may lead an interviewer to decide you are unwilling to take responsibility for any issues.

6. **DO NOT perform.** Unless you are asked to do so, steer clear of performing or auditioning. If you are asked to perform though, do not hold back.

AUDITION TIPS

1. **Take the earliest audition time possible.** At the end of the day, the casting team is tired and wants to go home. You don't want to be the one thing that stands in the way of that. Choosing the early time also means there is no one yet to compare you to.

2. **First impressions count.** Look professional. Sound professional. Be professional.

3. **Always bring a picture and resume.** Even if you, your agent, and your manager sent one ahead of the audition, bring them anyway.

4. **Don't pretend you memorized the material.** They'd rather have you read the lines than hear you make up lines just to show that you failed to memorize the material.

5. **Don't make excuses.** No one wants to hear that you have a cold, or that you didn't sleep well, or that blah blah blah. And, don't start over. If you make a mistake, just go on.

6. **Audition, audition, audition!** The more you audition, the better you'll be at it, so go for any and every audition you can until you land that part!

***

9 781978 187221